SUN YAT-SEN

SUN YAT-SEN

Jeffrey Barlow

CHELSEA HOUSE PUBLISHERS

NEW YORK

NEW HAVEN   PHILADELPHIA

EDITOR-IN-CHIEF: Nancy Toff
EXECUTIVE EDITOR: Remmel T. Nunn
MANAGING EDITOR: Karyn Gullen Browne
COPY CHIEF: Perry Scott King
ART DIRECTOR: Giannella Garrett
PICTURE EDITOR: Elizabeth Terhune

Staff for SUN YAT-SEN:

SENIOR EDITOR: John W. Selfridge
ASSISTANT EDITORS: Maria Behan, Pierre Hauser, Kathleen McDermott, Bert Yaeger
COPY EDITORS: Gillian Bucky, Sean Dolan
DESIGN ASSISTANT: Jill Goldreyer
PICTURE RESEARCH: Karen Herman
LAYOUT: David Murray
PRODUCTION COORDINATOR: Alma Rodriguez
COVER ILLUSTRATION: Kye Carbone

CREATIVE DIRECTOR: Harold Steinberg

Frontispiece courtesy of Xinhua News Agency

First Printing

Library of Congress Cataloging in Publication Data

Barlow, Jeffrey G. SUN YAT-SEN

(World leaders past & present)
Bibliography: p.
Includes index.
1. Sun, Yat-sen, 1866–1925— Juvenile literature.
2. China—Presidents—Biography— Juvenile literature.
[1. Sun, Yat-sen, 1866–1925. 2. Heads of state. 3. China—
History—1912–1928] I. Title. II. Series.
DS777.B35   1987   951.04′1′0924 [B] [92]   86-31732

ISBN 0-82254-441-7

Contents

CHELSEA HOUSE PUBLISHERS

WORLD LEADERS PAST & PRESENT

ON LEADERSHIP
Arthur M. Schlesinger, jr.

LEADERSHIP, it may be said, is really what makes the world go round. Love no doubt smooths the passage; but love is a private transaction between consenting adults. Leadership is a public transaction with history. The idea of leadership affirms the capacity of individuals to move, inspire, and mobilize masses of people so that they act together in pursuit of an end. Sometimes leadership serves good purposes, sometimes bad; but whether the end is benign or evil, great leaders are those men and women who leave their personal stamp on history.

Now, the very concept of leadership implies the proposition that individuals can make a difference. This proposition has never been universally accepted. From classical times to the present day, eminent thinkers have regarded individuals as no more than the agents and pawns of larger forces, whether the gods and goddesses of the ancient world or, in the modern era, race, class, nation, the dialectic, the will of the people, the spirit of the times, history itself. Against such forces, the individual dwindles into insignificance.

So contends the thesis of historical determinism. Tolstoy's great novel *War and Peace* offers a famous statement of the case. Why, Tolstoy asked, did millions of men in the Napoleonic wars, denying their human feelings and their common sense, move back and forth across Europe slaughtering their fellows? "The war," Tolstoy answered, "was bound to happen simply because it was bound to happen." All prior history predetermined it. As for leaders, they, Tolstoy said, "are but the labels that serve to give a name to an end and, like labels, they have the least possible connection with the event." The greater the leader, "the more conspicuous the inevitability and the predestination of every act he commits." The leader, said Tolstoy, is "the slave of history."

Determinism takes many forms. Marxism is the determinism of class. Nazism the determinism of race. But the idea of men and women as the slaves of history runs athwart the deepest human instincts. Rigid determinism abolishes the idea of human freedom—

the assumption of free choice that underlies every move we make, every word we speak, every thought we think. It abolishes the idea of human responsibility, since it is manifestly unfair to reward or punish people for actions that are by definition beyond their control. No one can live consistently by any deterministic creed. The Marxist states prove this themselves by their extreme susceptibility to the cult of leadership.

More than that, history refutes the idea that individuals make no difference. In December 1931 a British politician crossing Park Avenue in New York City between 76th and 77th Streets around 10:30 P.M. looked in the wrong direction and was knocked down by an automobile—a moment, he later recalled, of a man aghast, a world aglare: "I do not understand why I was not broken like an eggshell or squashed like a gooseberry." Fourteen months later an American politician, sitting in an open car in Miami, Florida, was fired on by an assassin; the man beside him was hit. Those who believe that individuals make no difference to history might well ponder whether the next two decades would have been the same had Mario Constasino's car killed Winston Churchill in 1931 and Giuseppe Zangara's bullet killed Franklin Roosevelt in 1933. Suppose, in addition, that Adolf Hitler had been killed in the street fighting during the Munich *Putsch* of 1923 and that Lenin had died of typhus during World War I. What would the 20th century be like now?

For better or for worse, individuals do make a difference. "The notion that a people can run itself and its affairs anonymously," wrote the philosopher William James, "is now well known to be the silliest of absurdities. Mankind does nothing save through initiatives on the part of inventors, great or small, and imitation by the rest of us—these are the sole factors in human progress. Individuals of genius show the way, and set the patterns, which common people then adopt and follow."

Leadership, James suggests, means leadership in thought as well as in action. In the long run, leaders in thought may well make the greater difference to the world. But, as Woodrow Wilson once said, "Those only are leaders of men, in the general eye, who lead in action. . . . It is at their hands that new thought gets its translation into the crude language of deeds." Leaders in thought often invent in solitude and obscurity, leaving to later generations the tasks of imitation. Leaders in action—the leaders portrayed in this series—have to be effective in their own time.

And they cannot be effective by themselves. They must act in response to the rhythms of their age. Their genius must be adapted, in a phrase of William James's, "to the receptivities of the moment." Leaders are useless without followers. "There goes the mob," said the French politician hearing a clamor in the streets. "I am their leader. I must follow them." Great leaders turn the inchoate emotions of the mob to purposes of their own. They seize on the opportunities of their time, the hopes, fears, frustrations, crises, potentialities. They succeed when events have prepared the way for them, when the community is awaiting to be aroused, when they can provide the clarifying and organizing ideas. Leadership ignites the circuit between the individual and the mass and thereby alters history.

It may alter history for better or for worse. Leaders have been responsible for the most extravagant follies and most monstrous crimes that have beset suffering humanity. They have also been vital in such gains as humanity has made in individual freedom, religious and racial tolerance, social justice and respect for human rights.

There is no sure way to tell in advance who is going to lead for good and who for evil. But a glance at the gallery of men and women in *World Leaders—Past and Present* suggests some useful tests.

One test is this: do leaders lead by force or by persuasion? By command or by consent? Through most of history leadership was exercised by the divine right of authority. The duty of followers was to defer and to obey. "Theirs not to reason why,/ Theirs but to do and die." On occasion, as with the so-called "enlightened despots" of the 18th century in Europe, absolutist leadership was animated by humane purposes. More often, absolutism nourished the passion for domination, land, gold and conquest and resulted in tyranny.

The great revolution of modern times has been the revolution of equality. The idea that all people should be equal in their legal condition has undermined the old structure of authority, hierarchy and deference. The revolution of equality has had two contrary effects on the nature of leadership. For equality, as Alexis de Tocqueville pointed out in his great study *Democracy in America*, might mean equality in servitude as well as equality in freedom.

"I know of only two methods of establishing equality in the political world," Tocqueville wrote. "Rights must be given to every citizen, or none at all to anyone . . . save one, who is the master of all." There was no middle ground "between the sovereignty of all and the absolute power of one man." In his astonishing prediction of 20th-century totalitarian dictatorship, Tocqueville explained how the revolution of equality could lead to the *"Führerprinzip"* and more terrible absolutism than the world had ever known.

But when rights are given to every citizen and the sovereignty of all is established, the problem of leadership takes a new form, becomes more exacting than ever before. It is easy to issue commands and enforce them by the rope and the stake, the concentration camp and the *gulag.* It is much harder to use argument and achievement to overcome opposition and win consent. The Founding Fathers of the United States understood the difficulty. They believed that history had given them the opportunity to decide, as Alexander Hamilton wrote in the first Federalist Paper, whether men are indeed capable of basing government on "reflection and choice, or whether they are forever destined to depend . . . on accident and force."

Government by reflection and choice called for a new style of leadership and a new quality of followership. It required leaders to be responsive to popular concerns, and it required followers to be active and informed participants in the process. Democracy does not eliminate emotion from politics; sometimes it fosters demagoguery; but it is confident that, as the greatest of democratic leaders put it, you cannot fool all of the people all of the time. It measures leadership by results and retires those who overreach or falter or fail.

It is true that in the long run despots are measured by results too. But they can postpone the day of judgment, sometimes indefinitely, and in the meantime they can do infinite harm. It is also true that democracy is no guarantee of virtue and intelligence in government, for the voice of the people is not necessarily the voice of God. But democracy, by assuring the right of opposition, offers built-in resistance to the evils inherent in absolutism. As the theologian Reinhold Niebuhr summed it up, "Man's capacity for justice makes democracy possible, but man's inclination to injustice makes democracy necessary."

A second test for leadership is the end for which power is sought. When leaders have as their goal the supremacy of a master race or the promotion of totalitarian revolution or the acquisition and exploitation of colonies or the protection of greed and privilege or the preservation of personal power, it is likely that their leadership will do little to advance the cause of humanity. When their goal is the abolition of slavery, the liberation of women, the enlargement of opportunity for the poor and powerless, the extension of equal rights to racial minorities, the defense of the freedoms of expression and opposition, it is likely that their leadership will increase the sum of human liberty and welfare.

Leaders have done great harm to the world. They have also conferred great benefits. You will find both sorts in this series. Even "good" leaders must be regarded with a certain wariness. Leaders are not demigods; they put on their trousers one leg after another just like ordinary mortals. No leader is infallible, and every leader needs to be reminded of this at regular intervals. Irreverence irritates leaders but is their salvation. Unquestioning submission corrupts leaders and demands followers. Making a cult of a leader is always a mistake. Fortunately hero worship generates its own antidote. "Every hero," said Emerson, "becomes a bore at last."

The signal benefit the great leaders confer is to embolden the rest of us to live according to our own best selves, to be active, insistent, and resolute in affirming our own sense of things. For great leaders attest to the reality of human freedom against the supposed inevitabilities of history. And they attest to the wisdom and power that may lie within the most unlikely of us, which is why Abraham Lincoln remains the supreme example of great leadership. A great leader, said Emerson, exhibits new possibilities to all humanity. "We feed on genius. . . . Great men exist that there may be greater men."

Great leaders, in short, justify themselves by emancipating and empowering their followers. So humanity struggles to master its destiny, remembering with Alexis de Tocqueville: "It is true that around every man a fatal circle is traced beyond which he cannot pass; but within the wide verge of that circle he is powerful and free; as it is with man, so with communities."

1

The Passing of the Old Order

China was in turmoil as 1911 ended. The reigning Qing dynasty, which had ruled the country since 1644, was about to fall from power. The political system known as dynasticism, whereby ruling families passed on the throne from generation to generation, had endured in China for more than 2,000 years. Now, however, a new form of government was emerging.

The most formidable of the many ambitious men who wanted to secure supremacy over that new government was General Yuan Shikai, the powerful warlord who led the Qing armies. Yuan controlled much of northern China from his base in Beijing (the Chinese capital; formerly known as Peking) and enjoyed the complete confidence of the emperor, Xuantong, who was fully prepared to follow Yuan's recommendation that he abdicate in the interests of national unity. Yuan also had a major advantage over his competitors in that he was backed by the foreign diplomatic corps in China. This was a vitally important consideration, since the new government stood little chance of surviving unless it was recognized by the United States, France, Great Britain,

> *To understand is hard.*
> *Once one understands,*
> *action is easy.*
> —SUN YAT-SEN

Cultural China in the early 1900s. An official pigtail cutter smiles for the camera after he snips the traditional braid from the head of a young man. At the time, the pigtail was a symbol of subservience; to cut it was an act of defiance.

General Yuan Shikai, an ambitious and powerful warlord. As leader of the Qing government's armies and a confidant of the emperor, Xuantong, Yuan used his political advantage when competing with Sun Yat-sen for the leadership of the Chinese Republic.

Germany, Japan, and Russia. Those countries had recently secured a virtual stranglehold on the Chinese economy and were thus in a position to destroy easily any Chinese government that failed to comply with their wishes. But Yuan, despite his willingness to accommodate the European powers, still faced serious problems.

While Yuan had been consolidating his position in the north, southern China had come under the control of a coalition of rebel groups which, while lacking coordination and clear direction, had nevertheless managed to present an effective challenge to the Qing dynasty. Based in Nanjing, a major city on the Changjiang (Yangtze) River, the southern rebel forces included mutinous soldiers, groups of conspiratorial students, and secret societies made up of violent, disaffected peasants who were little more than bandits.

The southern rebels, convinced that Yuan Shikai was planning to make himself emperor, were violently opposed to the prospect of national unification under northern command. They favored a new and modern form of government, a republic, modeled on Western democracies. Somehow, they had to choose one man who would not only be able to unify and lead them, but who would also be acceptable to the foreign powers.

On December 29, 1911, representatives of the major southern rebel groups elected Dr. Sun Yat-sen provisional president of the Chinese Republic. Sun seemed to many to be an unlikely choice. A medical doctor by profession, he was not a physically impressive, martial figure like Yuan Shikai, but a slightly built, quiet, and unassuming man of medium height. Unlike most prominent Chinese of his time, who were versed in Chinese classical learning and came from affluent families, Sun came from a peasant family and had received a Western education.

Sun was also much different from his fellow revolutionaries in that he had spent much of his life outside China and was a devout Christian. In fact, he was so well acquainted with Western politics and culture that some of his friends doubted that he was still truly Chinese. And now this mild-mannered physician who seemed almost a foreigner in his own country had been chosen to transform the volatile rebel coalition into a stable and viable political force, to come to terms with General Yuan Shikai, and to tackle the problems that had brought China to the brink of anarchy.

While much had changed in China over the more than 2,000 years during which it had been governed by imperial dynasties, Chinese society's most enduring characteristic — fundamental social and political inequalities — had remained constant. A very few people, perhaps 20 million out of a total population of 400 million, were relatively well off. Labeled the "scholar-gentry" by early Western visitors to China, they were highly educated and possessed powers and privileges similar to those enjoyed by

Sun Yat-sen opposed the Manchu regime as a young man and eventually became the leader of the Chinese United League, paving the way for the overthrow of the old imperial order.

XINHUA NEWS AGENCY

A portrait of a Chinese mandarin and his wife in 17th-century China. The vast majority of the Chinese population were impoverished peasants, but a small number of mandarins, or scholar-gentry, dominated the social, political, and economic order in prerevolutionary China.

European aristocrats (who also owned land and dominated the socioeconomic order). They were responsible for the administration of the governmental apparatus at all levels — national, regional, and local — and thus exercised complete control of political and economic affairs. Another, more popular name for them was "mandarins."

The rest of the population, however, were poor peasants. If they were so fortunate as to have their own farm, it would be very small, usually less than one-half acre. Most peasants farmed someone else's land, paying a fixed rent that generally amounted to one-half or more of the crop grown in a good year. Even when the harvest was very poor, tenant farmers had to pay the landlord the fixed rent before taking their own share. When conditions were favorable, most Chinese were able at least to subsist. But when droughts and floods — to which China has long been prone — ravaged the country, millions of peasants would die in the famines that followed.

Despite periodic problems in China, there had been few instances of popular agitation for social change. The country's political stability was entirely due to the resilience of its governmental institutions, which were designed to reflect the precepts of Confucianism, the philosophy in which the scholar-gentry were versed. Named for its originator, the 6th-century B.C. Chinese philosopher Confucius, Confucianism (which is essentially concerned with ethics and morality) holds that people can realize a state of heavenly harmony by cultivating certain virtues, including obedience, sincerity, and knowledge. Confucianism also holds that the realization of this state is greatly aided when children and parents as well as subjects and rulers fulfill their obligations toward each other.

According to Confucian philosophy, the emperors ruled by virtue of their having been accorded the "Mandate of Heaven." In the context of this doctrine, the Chinese held that natural disasters such as floods, famines, and epidemics were signs that heaven was displeased with the ruling dynasty and intended another order to assume the mandate.

Famine in China. People are shown dying of starvation here as a result of devastating droughts and floods that ravaged the country and crippled China's agricultural production in 1920.

Over the centuries, the Confucian bureaucratic system had provided security and stability on a scale that was unmatched in other premodern societies. Emperors and dynasties rose and fell, but the system as a whole survived. Historians believe that by most measures China's level of civilization remained qualitatively superior to the level that had been achieved in Europe until perhaps as late as the mid-18th century. More books circulated in China, and a higher percentage of the population was literate, than was the case in Europe during the same period. The imperial examination system, whereby educated males were tested in their knowledge of Confucian classical learning and, if successful, awarded posts as civil service administrators, provided the Chinese with greater opportunities for advancement than those that were available to most Europeans.

It was not until the middle of the Qing era that the Confucian bureaucratic system found itself confronted with a series of problems that strained its capabilities to the breaking point. Ironically, these problems were, to some extent, of its own making. The efficiency with which the bureaucracy had administered the agrarian production process resulted in a considerable increase in agricultural output. As the country prospered, its population increased dramatically, rising from around 150 million at the end of the 17th century to approximately 430 million by 1850. As historian Harold Z. Schiffrin explains in his book *Sun Yat-sen: Reluctant Revolutionary*, "The gap between productive capacity and population narrowed dangerously. This kind of crisis, which was . . . not merely administrative, could not be managed by refurbishing the old order under new leadership." By the middle of the 19th century it had become apparent that the crisis could only be resolved by industrialization and modernization. Such a transformation, however, would entail the importation of Western technology and ideas, a prospect that the majority of China's ruling elite found almost impossible to contemplate. Their ingrained tendency to regard all things Western as barbaric, along with their typi-

Chinese woodcut of the arrival of one of the earliest European steamboats and its passengers in Guangzhou in the 1840s. Since the early 16th century, merchants from major European powers such as Great Britain, France, and Spain traveled to China determined to exploit her fabled riches.

cally Confucian dislike of radical change, would eventually be their undoing. The inadequacy of dynastic rule and the Confucian bureaucracy would become apparent to increasing numbers of people, who would begin to demand the revolutionary changes of which their rulers were so obviously afraid.

Another problem facing the Qing dynasty was popular resentment of its non-Chinese origins, which became increasingly widespread as China's situation worsened. The Qing were descended from the Manchus, a nation of warrior-nomads from

British and Chinese clashes over the sale of opium in China resulted in the Opium Wars. Here the Qing dynasty's navy fights British troops in January 1841 at Guangzhou Bay. The British were victorious and forced the Chinese to allow the sale of opium to continue.

Manchuria, which lies to the northeast of China proper. The Manchus (who had established the Qing regime in 1636) conquered the Chinese capital in 1644. They overthrew the Ming dynasty (which had ruled since 1368), and founded the Qing dynasty, which is also referred to as the Manchu-Qing or the Manchu dynasty.

The Manchus ruled China in much the same way that their indigenous predecessors had done. They had adopted the Chinese bureaucratic system long before invading and, following their accession to power, soon adopted Chinese dress and customs and conducted court business in the Chinese language. This approach enabled them to gain the support of the scholar-gentry, who in turn declared the Qing possessors of the all-important divine mandate. China's elite thus followed Confucian tradition, showing itself less concerned with its rulers' ethnic origins than with the new dynasty's commitment to the preservation of China's culture and institutions. For many Chinese, however, the Qing remained outsiders. The majority ethnic group in China (about 95 percent of the population) were known as the Han. Many of those who rebelled against the Qing, including Sun Yat-sen, sought to exploit the anti-Manchu sentiments of the Han majority in their endeavors to move the Hans to overthrow the Qing dynasty.

In addition to the problems of popular resentment of their foreign origins and of presiding over an administration that was having trouble coping with the results of overpopulation, the Qing also had to meet new threats from the encroaching Western powers and from the Japanese. Beginning with the Portuguese in the early 16th century, increasing numbers of European merchants were drawn to China, hoping to exploit the country's fabled riches. The major European powers of the time — Portugal, Spain, the Netherlands, France, Great Britain, and Russia — were eager to expand their economic bases and began to seek profits abroad through colonization and maritime trade. This expansion brought them to China at a time when that country was at its weakest point in many centuries.

The Europeans were determined to trade with China on the most favorable terms possible. The Chinese government, however, was equally determined to establish conditions for contact that reflected its sense of superiority and self-sufficiency. The Europeans were initially given access to China at just two points — Guangzhou (formerly Canton), a port in the southern province of Guangdong, and Macao, a small peninsula on the western edge of the Xijiang River delta, also in southern China. Guangdong, which was the economic center of southern China, was also Sun Yat-sen's native province.

The British, who began trading at Guangzhou in 1699, soon found themselves confronting a serious trade imbalance. The Chinese government had no intention of allowing British goods onto the Chinese market and required that the British pay for their

China is not the colony of one nation but of all, and we are not the slaves of one country but of all.
—SUN YAT-SEN

When the Taipings were defeated by the Manchu forces in 1864, the victors were equipped with a fairly modernized army. Still, this Chinese imperial soldier carries breech-loading cartridges around his waist, a type of ammunition that is of absolutely no use for the old type matchlock like the one he is holding.

purchases of Chinese tea, silk, and timber with silver, rather than by an exchange of goods. Britain was thus buying far more from China than it was selling to her and was soon forced to resort to increased taxation, both at home and in its colonies, as a means of redressing the imbalance. The tea thrown into Boston harbor by the angry American colonists in 1773 was Chinese tea, and the taxes that the Americans were protesting were intended to help pay for the costs of the tea trade. However, none of the measures the British adopted solved the problem of the trade imbalance with China.

Early in the 19th century the British changed tactics and began exploiting a product that seemed likely to become the answer to their problems — opium. Easily and cheaply grown in British colonies (particularly in India), this powerfully addictive drug was smuggled into Guangdong by unscrupulous British merchants, who rapidly made vast fortunes. The more the Chinese bought, the more they wanted.

The Manchu government, which considered trade with foreigners neither necessary nor desirable, was profoundly disturbed by the British attempt to secure an economic advantage by turning China into a nation of drug addicts. The British, for their part, felt that the Chinese trading system, which was tightly regulated by the central government, had prevented them from turning a profit legally and that the opium trade represented their only alternative to abandoning all attempts to penetrate the Chinese market. Both sides were playing for very high stakes, and when the Chinese government attempted to enforce its anti-opium laws, Britain went to war in defense of its own vision of free commerce, launching a series of short and brutal conflicts that became known as the Opium Wars, the first of which was fought between 1839 and 1842. As an industrializing power, Britain had a massive technological advantage over the Chinese. Her warships, which carried modern guns and could land detachments of troops armed with new, rapid-fire rifles, proved unbeatable. The British emerged victorious and forced the Chinese government to permit the

opium trade. As a result, the economic imbalance that had triggered the British aggression was quickly reversed. Increasingly greater amounts of Chinese silver flowed into the coffers of British trading concerns and merchant banks, while opium addiction became a widespread problem in many parts of China.

In the wake of Britain's victories, the other European nations began to compete for expanded commercial privileges in the few Chinese ports where the Chinese government permitted foreign traders to operate. The Chinese government deferred its plans for bolstering the country's defenses and decided instead to pursue a policy of appeasement toward the European powers. China made numerous concessions to European interests, even granting its approval of extraterritoriality, whereby foreigners were made immune from prosecution under Chinese law and could enjoy the protection of foreign courts on Chinese soil.

Rebel soldiers who fought to overthrow the Qing dynasty during the Taiping Rebellion (1850–1864). The Taiping revolutionaries were attempting to set up a new political system based on communal ownership of property.

By 1895, when Sun Yat-sen planned his first armed action against the Qing, even the minor Western powers had gained commercial footholds (and associated extraterritorial privileges) in China's treaty ports. The British had secured complete control of the Chinese maritime customs service, which meant that China could not use tariffs to protect her own economy from cheap foreign goods. In northern China, American, German, Russian, and Japanese interests vied for control over profitable banking, railroad, and mining operations. Japan and Russia were competing for regional supremacy in Manchuria and Mongolia, and foreign powers had also established colonial regimes in Tibet and Annam (now part of Vietnam), both of which had previously been Chinese dependencies. The Qing and the scholar-statesmen who administered their empire proved incapable of halting the steady erosion of Chinese sovereignty.

Between 1850 and 1900 domestic opposition to the Manchu government became increasingly widespread. Overpopulation and the government's inability to provide adequate relief in the wake of natural disasters had begun to provoke the peasantry beyond endurance. There were many attempts to overthrow the Manchu-Qing, the most notable of which was the great Taiping Rebellion, which raged throughout China from 1850 until 1864 and caused at least 20 million deaths. (Some estimates put the

Buddhist priests take part in a religious ceremony in 1890. Chinese peasants remained faithful to long-established religions such as Buddhism, which had spread from India to China in the 3rd century A.D.

THE BETTMANN ARCHIVE

death toll as high as 40 million.) This staggering loss of life demonstrated that China's capacity to feed itself was now utterly dependent on continued social stability: most of the fatalities resulted from starvation due to the disruption of the cycle of planting and harvesting rather than from battle.

The name "Taiping" is often translated as "The Heavenly Kingdom of Great Peace." The Taiping rebels were influenced by Christian notions that they had learned from Western missionaries and of which they had only an imperfect understanding. The Taiping movement's founder, Hong Xiuquan, believed himself to be the younger brother of Jesus Christ and thought the Manchus were human incarnations of the Christian devil.

The Taiping wanted more than a new emperor or a new dynasty; they wanted an entirely new political system, modeled on the one that had purportedly existed during China's mythical "Golden Age." But the Taiping were never to realize their vision of a totalitarian state where all property would be held under common ownership. Their leaders, who were not drawn from the scholar-gentry class, proved to be poor administrators. They were incapable of instituting effective government in the territories they occupied and failed to develop a strong economic or political base. Their foreign-influenced religious ideas were utterly alien to the peasants, who preferred traditional Chinese Buddhism or Taoism. The mandarin class, thoroughly disturbed by the Taiping rebels' extremism, rallied to the Qing and assumed local military responsibilities to defeat the insurgents. The foreign powers, convinced that the Taiping were not really Christian and posed a greater threat to foreign rights and privileges in China than did the weak Manchu government, decided to support the ruling dynasty. Finally, in 1864, the Qing armies inflicted a decisive defeat on the Taiping forces.

Two years later, while southern China was still recovering from the effects of the rebellion, Sun Yat-sen was born in Guangdong province. He was to devote his life to the overthrow of the Qing regime and the creation of a Chinese republic.

XINHUA NEWS AGENCY

Hong Xiuquan, leader and founder of the Taiping movement. The Taiping rebels derived their political ideology from Christian missionaries in the mid-19th century. So strong was this influence that Hong Xiuquan believed himself to be Jesus Christ's younger brother.

2
Sun's Youth

Sun Yat-sen was born on November 12, 1866, in Cuiheng, a small village about 12 miles from Guangzhou, China's great southern port. His parents were peasants and farmed three acres rented from a landlord. The family farm was considerably larger than most in the region, and the Suns were, accordingly, relatively well-off by Chinese standards.

Sun had a conventional Chinese childhood. Like many young boys whose parents hoped to see their sons enter the socially prestigious Chinese civil service, he studied the Confucian classics. Sun also did light work in the fields, watched over ducks and chickens, and herded water buffalo.

The Sun family, like many in Guangdong province, had relatives abroad. Because life as a farmer rarely offered more than subsistence, and overpopulation was as much of a problem in Guangdong as it was elsewhere in China, many people had left the province hoping to make a livelihood overseas. Guangzhou, which had been a major port for centuries, was their main point of departure.

Those who emigrated were known as overseas Chinese. If they settled down and became citizens in a foreign country, they were properly referred to

I am a coolie, the son of a coolie.
—SUN YAT-SEN

A typical river scene in Guangzhou, China, in 1926. During this time nearly half a million of the city's inhabitants lived on river boats, going ashore only on rare occasions.

Set against a mountain backdrop in Guangdong Province is Cuiheng village, the birthplace of Sun Yat-sen. The Sun household included three acres of land, which the family farmed.

as Chinese Americans or Canadian Chinese, depending on their new place of residence. By 1900 there were almost no large cities in the world without overseas Chinese communities. The largest overseas Chinese communities were in Annam and the British colony of Singapore, the wealthiest in Hawaii and California. Natives of Guangdong province were, in many respects, the most conspicuous element of that portion of the Chinese population that had come into contact with Europeans and other Westerners, both overseas and in the treaty ports.

Two of Sun Yat-sen's uncles had gone to the United States in the middle of the 19th century, when, in the wake of the California Gold Rush of 1848 and the development of railroads and mines in the American West, there was great demand for cheap Chinese labor in that country. During the latter half of the 19th century, roughly 120,000 Guangdong natives left the province every year to work as coolies (laborers) in Southeast Asia and the Americas. Conditions aboard the coolie ships were generally appalling, and it was not unusual for up to 20 percent of a coolie ship's passengers to die during the voyage. The Sun family eventually learned that one of the brothers had died at sea, and the other in the California gold fields. And yet, because the amount of money a Chinese could make overseas was so staggeringly great by the standards of his poverty-stricken homeland, members of the Sun family continued to seek their fortunes abroad.

One of these relatives was Sun's older brother, Sun Mei, who proved luckier than his paternal uncles. He arrived in Hawaii in 1871, when the island's sugar industry was beginning to expand. He worked as a laborer, saved his money, and eventually ac-

Chinese mining for gold in California. In the late 1800s many Chinese journeyed abroad to escape the impoverished conditions in their own country and to seek what they hoped would be a higher standard of living. In the United States Chinese workers were exploited as a cheap source of labor.

Coolies in central China. During the late 19th century, Chinese peasants were transported by foreign powers to work abroad, but many never reached their destinations. Conditions aboard coolie ships were wretched, causing many deaths at sea.

quired some farmland and became owner of a store. Sun Mei also became a labor broker, returning to China at regular intervals to recruit new workers, paying their passage to Hawaii and receiving as compensation a percentage of the workers' commissions from the plantation owners. When Sun Mei made his first return trip to China, in 1877, the people of Cuiheng village treated him with great respect. He had been sending substantial amounts of money home, and, as a result, his family had come to enjoy increased social prominence. Sun was entranced by his older brother's stories of life in Hawaii and begged to be allowed to accompany Sun Mei back there. His parents refused, declaring that Sun Yat-sen was too young to make such a move.

Two years later, when Sun was 12, his parents permitted him to join Sun Mei in Honolulu. This was Sun Yat-sen's first trip outside his village, and he was fascinated by his first encounter with Western customs and culture.

Because Sun's brother was relatively wealthy, Sun, unlike most Chinese expatriates, did not have to work for a living. His brother sent him to Iolani College, a secondary school for boys of Hawaiian birth that was run by Church of England clergymen. Because Sun was an Oriental, he had to attend school with Hawaiian boys and not with the children of the American community in Honolulu.

The years from the age of 12 to 16 are very important ones in any person's life. In Sun Yat-sen's case, they were particularly formative. For it was in Hawaii that he learned to speak English and began to acquire the Western education and the familiarity with foreigners and foreign ideas that would distinguish him from the other Chinese political leaders of his generation. Later, when Sun traveled the world seeking financial and political backing for the Chinese revolution from Americans, Englishmen, and Frenchmen, much of what he had learned during his time at Iolani College would prove invaluable.

A busy street scene in Honolulu, Hawaii, in the early 20th century. Sun Yat-sen, who would make many trips to Hawaii during his lifetime, first went there in 1879 to live with his older brother, Sun Mei. There he learned lessons that later in his life would prove invaluable in his dealings with leaders of powerful Western nations.

French troops enter Hanoi, the capital of the Southeast Asian kingdom of Tonkin, in April 1883. The Tonkinese and their Chinese allies were defeated in the Sino-French War, and Tonkin became part of France's colonial empire in Indochina.

It was also at Iolani College that Sun, much to his brother's dismay, became attracted to Christianity. Sun Mei, as an important member of the Chinese community, had no intention of allowing his younger brother to make such a radical break with tradition. After Sun graduated from Iolani College, he spent several months working with Sun Mei, who was by now a successful planter, rancher, and merchant. However, Sun found business rather boring and soon asked to be allowed to resume his studies. He attended Oahu College, which was run by American Congregationalist and Presbyterian missionaries, for about a year, until the middle of 1883. His announcement that he was to be baptized as a Christian prompted Sun Mei to remove him from further foreign influence by sending him back to China.

Shortly after Sun returned to Cuiheng, his family decided that he should marry. Sun was 17 at the time, and it was not unusual for Chinese boys to marry at that age. Since his brother intended to stay in Hawaii indefinitely, Sun was now the successor to his father, traditionally an important responsibility in China.

Marriage was a very important event, not so much to the individuals concerned, who often did not even see their spouses before the ceremony, but to the two families, who were mingling their fortunes through marriage. As a result, arranging a suitably beneficial and profitable match usually involved extensive negotiations. And it was while Sun's family was conducting such negotiations that the young man whose future they were debating got into serious trouble in his home village.

Sun always enjoyed close friendships with other progressive boys of his own age, and he and one of these boys deliberately damaged a wooden statue of the Northern God, the patron deity of Cuiheng. This act was a grave affront to local religion and had the effect of further antagonizing the village elders, who were already intensely resentful of Sun's tendency to regard himself as superior to everybody else in the village because he had a Western education. Sun was also disliked by the villagers because he had tried to become a Christian.

Sun's desecration of the holy statue also had political overtones. It was common knowledge that Hong Xiuquan, the founder of the Taiping movement, had first attained notoriety by perpetrating a similar act. Many of the Taiping rebels had come from Sun's district, and it seemed that Sun was aligning himself with a very subversive tradition.

Sun's family decided that he should leave the village until preparations for his marriage were complete. They sent him to the adjoining British colony of Hong Kong, where he resumed his education and began to take an increasing interest in politics.

Chinese and American doctors and medical students in Guangzhou. Dr. John Kerr (seated, fourth from left) was director of the Guangzhou Hospital Medical School, where Sun Yat-sen gained admission in 1886 to study medicine.

In 1883, while Sun was studying in Hong Kong, French troops invaded Tonkin, a tributary state of China in Southeast Asia. The Chinese and Tonkinese gave a good account of themselves in the guerrilla war that ensued, but the conflict was ultimately decided by French naval power. French warships bombarded southern China's ports and also destroyed a modern Chinese shipyard on the island province of Taiwan. In 1884—85 French troops carried the war onto Chinese soil, invading the southern provinces of Guangxi, Fujian, and Zhejiang. The Chinese armies fought bravely but were unable to check the French advance. The Qing government, considering further resistance useless, capitulated in June 1885, and Tonkin became a part of French Indochina.

It was during the Sino-French War that Sun had his first encounter with the patriotism of the Chinese working class. In September 1884 a French warship that had taken part in an attack on a Chinese port put into Hong Kong for repairs. The Chinese dockworkers immediately went on strike and refused to service the ship. Further industrial action followed; Hong Kong harbor was closed down for several days and the French vessel eventually sailed to Japan for repairs.

It was also during the Sino-French War that Sun's family arranged a suitable match for him. In May 1884 he married a young girl named Lu Szu, with whom he was to have a son and two daughters. He would, however, spend most of his time away from his family, engaged in political activities. China's deteriorating fortunes in the war with France had served further to convince Sun that the Manchu government was hopelessly inept and utterly incapable of protecting China's interests against the depredations of the foreign powers. He returned to Hong Kong.

In Hong Kong, Sun was finally baptized into the Christian faith. The American Congregationalist missionary who officiated at the ceremony, Dr. Charles R. Hager, was to be a good friend to the young Chinese convert. During this period Sun began to consider what kind of career he should follow, and at one point even considered becoming a Christian minister. Finally, in 1886, Sun decided that he could best serve his country by becoming a medical doctor.

In 1886 Dr. Hager helped Sun gain admission to the Guangzhou Hospital Medical School, whose director, an American named Dr. John Kerr, had a reputation as a leading advocate of the introduction of modern medicine into China. In Guangzhou, Sun also spent much time engaging in heated political discussions with other young Chinese progressives, including some who had connections with the Triads, the largest and most powerful of the southern Chinese secret societies. The secret societies, which had proliferated throughout China, were peasant-dominated groups that sought to counter

From 1885, i.e., from the time of our defeat in the war with France, I set myself the object of the overthrow of the Qing dynasty and the establishment of a Chinese republic in its ruins.
—SUN YAT-SEN

the local power of the scholar-gentry. The secret societies also operated abroad, among the overseas Chinese communities, where they functioned as self-help organizations. One of the young Triad contacts with whom Sun associated in Guangzhou, a medical student named Zheng Shiliang, became one of Sun's closest friends and was to play a prominent role in Sun's early conspiracies against the Qing. Zheng's assurances to Sun that the Triads would be prepared to assist in an uprising planted the seeds of the young revolutionary's future willingness to forge alliances with the secret societies, even though he found many of their activities distasteful. It was common knowledge that the overseas lodges, or branches, of the secret societies had

Japanese troops storm a Chinese fort during the Sino-Japanese War, 1894—95. China's defeat further exposed the country's inability to repel attacks by modern industrialized nations and dramatized to many Chinese the need for social change.

taken self-help to rather dubious extremes and were heavily involved in prostitution and racketeering. Such activities had made the overseas lodges of the secret societies extremely wealthy, and the idea of securing financial backing from the secret societies was also to figure in Sun's calculations.

In 1887 Sun left Guangzhou to continue his medical training at the College of Medicine in Hong Kong. Sun did extremely well at his studies, and while he continued to play the revolutionary in the company of his friends, he began to suspect that he could make a greater contribution to the modernization of China as a Western-educated professional than he could as a rebel.

Many of the reformist ideas that Sun acquired

Sun (second from left) meets with fellow revolutionaries. Many young Chinese intellectuals attacked the corrupt rule of the Qing dynasty and the imperialist policies of Western nations.

while studying in Hong Kong resulted from his association with Dr. He Qi, one of the lecturers at the college. He Qi had written numerous newspaper articles in which he contended that the main problem confronting China was not the greed of the foreign powers but its own backwardness. And that backwardness, he believed, was due to the fact that the country's leaders were still being selected on the basis of their familiarity with Chinese classical knowledge. Such officials, he said, would never be able to transform China's institutions along Western lines. Only Western-educated Chinese — who would never be appointed to positions of authority while the imperial examination system remained in place — could manage such an undertaking. He Qi's tireless advocacy of Chinese modernization helped Sun realize that a Western-educated Chinese professional need not restrict himself to his chosen area of endeavor; he could also express his views on public issues.

Another relationship that meant a great deal to Sun during his time in Hong Kong was with Dr.

James Cantlie, who was appointed dean of the school in 1889. Dr. Cantlie became a close friend and had an important influence on Sun.

Sun graduated at the head of his class in 1892 but was unable to practice in Hong Kong because his qualifications did not match the requirements of the Hong Kong General Medical Council. Sun then went to the nearby Portuguese colony of Macao, where he established a practice that combined both Western medicine and traditional Chinese herbalism. The Portuguese authorities, however, refused to allow Sun to treat Portuguese patients. They also issued restrictions forbidding pharmacies to fill prescriptions for foreign doctors. Realizing that the racism of the Portuguese was making his situation impossible, Sun returned to China.

During 1894–95, China fought and lost yet another war with a foreign power. This time the victor was not a European state but Japan. Their defeat by Japan traumatized the Chinese much more profoundly than had their capitulation to France in 1885. Japan, formerly as backward as China in many ways, had transformed into a major Asian power (and had also begun to emerge as a prospective world power) in less than 40 years. Following its transformation into a constitutional monarchy with democratic institutions in 1889, Japan had embarked upon a crash program of continuing political reform, rapid industrialization, and military modernization. Japan's victory offered convincing evidence of the benefits of reform and made it painfully apparent that China had made little or no progress in comparison. The war also deprived China of part of its territory, the island province of Taiwan, which was ceded to Japan.

Like many Chinese, Sun Yat-sen was galvanized into action by this defeat. It seemed to him that unless the Chinese people acted quickly and overthrew the Manchus, China's nationality might be irretrievably lost. And it was at this critical juncture in his country's history that Sun Yat-sen started out upon the path of political activism that would eventually result in his being elected provisional president of the Chinese Republic.

He was the model and the example to the other members of the classes . . . he attracted by his personality both teachers and fellow students.
—DR. JAMES CANTLIE
dean of the College of
Medicine in Hong Kong

3

The Way of Revolution

Shortly after the outbreak of the Sino-Japanese War, Sun had decided that the time had come to create a revolutionary organization. Realizing that adequate financing would be a vital prerequisite for any such project, he went to Hawaii, hoping to secure assistance from his brother, Sun Mei, who had continued to prosper. Sun was also eager to exploit the anti-Manchu sympathies of Hawaii's formidable overseas Chinese population (which numbered approximately 20,000) and to persuade that population's wealthier members to give him monetary as well as moral support. This concentration on financing was to characterize Sun throughout his career. He was not the kind of revolutionary who envisages decades of underground organizing or protracted military campaigns. China, he felt, was already on the verge of being partitioned by the Western powers, and the revolution had to take place soon, while the country was still a single political entity. In Sun's estimation, only a quick revolution, based on strong financial support and precise calculations, could save China from complete destruction.

It was, then, with such considerations constantly preoccupying him, that Sun founded the Revive China Society (in Chinese, Xing Zhong Hui) in Hawaii on November 24, 1894. Most of its approx-

Again and again I asserted to myself, 'surely there must be some remedy against this wickedness of the mandarins.'
—SUN YAT-SEN

A group of Manchu men in the Chinese capital of Beijing. The Manchus invaded China in 1644 and ruled over the country for more than two and a half centuries. Sun attempted to use the anti-Manchu sentiment of overseas Chinese communities to organize resistance to the ruling Manchu-Qing dynasty.

imately 20 members were overseas Chinese who would contribute money, and sometimes their lives, to the cause of the Chinese revolution. Sun still considered the overseas Chinese (and especially the more educated among them, who were more receptive to modern ideas) the natural base for the Chinese revolution, even though he had discovered that few of them were as yet prepared to work for the overthrow of the Manchus. Some took little interest in politics, and many of those who did refused to become activists because they feared Manchu reprisals against their relatives back home in China.

In establishing the Revive China Society, Sun was also seeking to adapt Chinese tradition to suit his own political purposes. Sun hoped the organization would be much like the secret societies with which he had come into contact in Guangzhou.

Chinese peasant farmers irrigating their rice fields with a foot-powered paddle. Hoping to gain support for the peasants of China, who suffered under the inept administration of the Manchu government, Sun established a base for his revolutionary activities in the port city of Hong Kong in 1895.

The Chinese government waged many campaigns against Christians within the country. This cartoon shows some of the punishments inflicted on foreigners and native Christian converts who refused to abandon their religious faith.

In January 1895, Sun abruptly abandoned both his political work in Hawaii and his preparations for a fund-raising tour of overseas Chinese communities in the United States. China's armed forces were reeling before the Japanese onslaught, and Sun was convinced that the time to act had come. Popular disaffection had begun to become widespread throughout southern China even before the deterioration of the military situation. Peasants had rioted to protest heavy taxation and the inadequacy of government relief efforts in the wake of poor harvests and famine. As always happened during periods of peasant agitation, the secret societies were becoming more active. Hoping to exploit the situation, Sun went to Hong Kong, intending to make it his base of operations.

In Hong Kong, Sun was reunited with the friends he had made during his days as a medical student. Many of them declared their willingness to work for revolution and introduced him to a group of young, Western-educated Chinese who also believed that China's misfortunes were due to the ineptitude of the Manchus and the scholar-gentry. The leader of the group was an imposing and extremely capable man named Yang Quyun, who was five years Sun's senior. When Sun and Yang's groups merged to form the Hong Kong branch of the Revive China Society, the leadership post of the new organization was left unfilled in order to forestall the possibility of a clash between the two men.

The imperial family of Japan. Sun fled Hong Kong in 1895 and journeyed to Japan — a country he both feared and admired. The Japanese had successfully combined their traditional customs with the practices of the Western industrialized world, establishing themselves as a powerful Asian presence.

The new organization's program was much the same as the one that Sun had proclaimed in Hawaii. It warned that China was in danger of dismemberment by the foreign powers and could only be saved by modern leaders, who would make China wealthy and powerful by educating the people and using modern science to develop a strong technological and industrial base.

The program also invited foreigners to play a part in China's transformation. Although this invitation might seem unusual in light of what the foreign powers were then doing to China, it reflected Sun and Yang's belief that their movement would stand no chance of success if it showed hostility to foreigners. The revolution would be greatly aided if the foreign powers supported it, or, failing that, at least remained neutral. And modernizing China would, especially in the early stages, require foreign expertise and finance. A certain readiness to accommodate foreign interests whenever it seemed that so doing might help China was to characterize Sun throughout his career. It was often to result in his doing things that delighted his enemies, antagonized his allies, or simply made no sense to either. But Sun always knew exactly what he was doing and made no apologies for his chosen way of working. And the Revive China Society's invitation to foreigners was the first great example of this unique aspect of Sun's approach to revolutionary politics.

In April 1895, shortly after Sun and his colleagues had begun to lay their plans for an assault on the government offices in Guangzhou that would, they hoped, trigger uprisings throughout Guangdong and, eventually, throughout the rest of the country, the Sino-Japanese War ended with the signing of the Treaty of Shimonoseki. Under the terms of the treaty, China was forced to cede Taiwan province and to pay Japan $160 million in reparations. China had been thoroughly humiliated, and her people began to despair. Thousands of discharged Chinese soldiers were turning to banditry, terrorizing the civil population, and the secret societies (for whose assistance Sun and his colleagues were now canvassing) had stepped up their activities.

Once he was satisfied that things were proceeding smoothly in Hong Kong, Sun went to Guangzhou to supervise the work of the local branch of the Revive China Society. Arms were purchased, bombs fabricated, secret-society members and militant students recruited for the striking force. On the public front, Sun assumed the guise of a reformer, giving talks on such subjects as education and scientific agricultural methods. His old friend He Qi used his contacts at two influential, British-owned English-language newspapers in Hong Kong to persuade the editors to write in support of the revolutionaries.

Unfortunately for Sun and his fellow conspirators, their projected coup was never to materialize. Disaster befell them on the very day upon which they had intended to make their move — October 26, 1895. The Guangzhou police, acting on information received from Manchu agents in Hong Kong, closed in on Sun's headquarters. Sun escaped from Guangzhou with the police at his heels and made

In order to divert attention and keep a low profile while pursuing revolutionary activities, Sun abandoned his traditional Chinese style of dress for a Western suit, a European hair style, and a mustache.

his way to Hong Kong. Most of his colleagues were not as lucky: 70 were arrested, and 3 of them were later put to death. In Hong Kong, Sun was informed that he and his friends should leave immediately since Manchu agents were still scouring the city.

Realizing that their situation was hopeless, Sun and two of his associates took passage aboard the first available vessel, and, on November 12, 1895, disembarked at Kobe, Japan. Sun had thus arrived by chance in the country that he was to regard as an example to the rest of Asia — even when he found its policies deplorable — for much of his career. Like many other progressive Chinese, Sun was fascinated by the fact that Japan had managed successfully to combine tradition with modernity. Japan still had an imperial family, and the Japanese continued to believe that their emperor was descended from the Sun Goddess, Japan's patron deity. But Japan had also adopted a constitution, modelled on that of imperial Germany, and had modernized very rapidly.

A pagoda, or multistoried tower, in Guangzhou. In 1895 Sun's first attempt at organizing a rebellion against the Manchu government ended in failure in Guangzhou, and he was forced to flee abroad.

Japan's leaders had instituted a modernization program mainly because they feared that without one their country would, like China, fall victim to the European powers. Their other motives, however, had to do with more than simple self-preservation. Japan now intended to make itself the predominant nation in Asia, to exclude the European powers and to create its own colonial system embracing China and Korea. [Thus, the *China Mail* informed its readers that the "reform party" intended to achieve power "by peaceful means" if possible, and to "rid their country of the iniquitous system of misrule which has shut out China from Western influences, Western trade, and Western civilization." Directly reflecting Sun's willingness to accommodate foreign interests (and to deceive them if need be), the *China Mail* also announced that the reformers would welcome "British enterprises and capital" and that they were not proposing "to set up a republic."] It was this eagerness to increase its influence on the Asian mainland that accounted for Japan's readiness to give limited (and little-publicized) assistance to Chinese revolutionaries like Sun Yat-sen.

While in refuge in Japan during the last months of 1895, Sun made several fundamental decisions about his future course of action. First, he reconsidered the problems inherent in any attempt to bring about revolution. His initial effort had ended in failure, costing the lives of a number of his comrades. Future attempts, he realized, would have to be better planned, and would require more extensive organization and more substantial financing. Still convinced that the overseas Chinese communities could be made an effective base from which to launch a modern, democratic revolution in China, Sun decided that he would be well advised to undertake a comprehensive tour of the most important of those communities.

As part of his preparations for the tour Sun changed his appearance, hoping to throw Manchu agents (who were reportedly attempting to keep track of him) off the scent. He abandoned traditional Chinese dress, cut off his queue (the pigtail that

I had no trouble, when I let my hair and mustache grow, in passing for a Japanese. I admit that I owe a great deal to this circumstance, as otherwise I would not have escaped from many dangerous situations.
—SUN YAT-SEN

47

Karl Marx, the 19th-century German social philosopher and economist. Sun studied the works of Marx and other radical thinkers of the late 1800s while developing his own political philosophy for a nationalist China.

was the customary symbol of Chinese subservience to the Manchus), combed his hair in the European style, grew a mustache, and began to wear a Western suit. When the transformation was complete, Sun (whose disguise was also helped by the fact that he was darker-skinned than most of his compatriots) could easily pass for a Japanese.

From Japan, Sun went first to Hawaii, where his mother (now a widow) and his wife and two children had joined the wealthy Sun Mei. In June 1896, having been unable to breathe new life into the Hawaiian branch of the Revive China Society, Sun left for the United States, hoping to raise both money and recruits among that country's overseas Chinese communities.

In the United States, Sun used his secret-society connections to secure introductions to prominent local Chinese in the cities he visited. Although Sun generally received a polite hearing, he had little impact on the communities as a whole. His audiences were small, and the money he collected barely sufficed to get him from one city to the next. While his friends in Hong Kong and Guangdong had been impressed with his Western education, in the United States there were many Chinese who were just as progressive as Sun and, in some cases, much better educated than he was. His tour had done little to further the revolutionary cause. Sun therefore decided to take the advice of his old teacher, Dr. Cantlie, whom he had unexpectedly met in Hawaii shortly before leaving for the United States, and visit London, where Dr. and Mrs. Cantlie were now living. Sun had often thought that seeing Europe would enable him to improve his knowledge of current affairs and to gain a better understanding of the countries that China would have to emulate before she could hope to compete with them.

In September 1896 Sun sailed from New York to England. There, he would begin a thorough education in modern thought. He was also to come very close to losing his life to the vengeful Manchus.

Immediately upon arriving in London, Sun got in touch with the Cantlies, who found him lodgings not far from their own home. His new residence was also close to the Chinese legation, whose staff had already been alerted to Sun's presence in London by Chinese diplomats in the United States. Knowing that the British authorities had refused to comply with the Chinese government's request that he be extradited, Sun had no qualms about visiting the legation. He was longing for the company of fellow Chinese, and remained convinced that his disguise would continue to work. On October 10, 1896, Sun went to the legation under an assumed name and met with a government employee, a native of Guangdong. The two arranged to meet again the following day. When Sun returned, on October 11, he was arrested; the employee had informed his superiors of Sun's visit, and Sun was identified from the description the man had given.

Sun was informed that he would be sent to China to stand trial for his revolutionary activities and that he would certainly be sentenced to death. Sun pleaded with his captors, appealed for help to the legation's British employees, and even threw messages out the window of his room in hopes that passersby would find them. But, for 12 days, nothing worked. Finally, the wife of one of the British

A detachment of Red Guards assemble during the Russian Revolution of 1917. Organizations dedicated to overthrowing the government were active in both Russia and China in the 1890's. Marx's disciple Vladimir Lenin succeeded in creating a socialist state in Russia after the revolution.

After leaving England in 1897, Sun traveled to Canada and Japan. While in Japan, Sun (seated, second from left) met Torazo Miyazaki (standing, third from left), a Japanese pan-Asianist who supported Sun's revolutionary cause.

servants in the legation went to Dr. Cantlie's home and left an anonymous note, informing him of Sun's peril.

Cantlie had great difficulty in persuading the British police to concern themselves with Sun's predicament, which they regarded as "Chinese business" and, therefore, none of theirs. When Dr. Cantlie contacted officials at the British Foreign Office, he had no more luck than he had had with the police. Not wishing to antagonize the Manchu regime and thus risk jeopardizing the Anglo-Chinese treaty system (which was so much to Britain's advantage), the Foreign Office refused to get involved. Repeatedly frustrated in his attempts to secure help from the authorities, Dr. Cantlie finally took his case to a London newspaper, the *Globe*. The *Globe* featured the event as a major story and plastered London with advertising placards proclaiming "Chinese Revolutionary Kidnapped in London." The *Globe*'s coverage aroused the sympathies of the British people and got the attention of the authorities. Sun was released on October 23, 1896.

Sun exploited his unanticipated arrival at the center of public attention in Britain in a variety of ways, all of which were designed to further his own cause and to discredit the Manchus. He made a great impression on the reporters who interviewed him and wrote a letter to the London *Times* (which was then the most respected newspaper in Britain) in which he attributed his salvation to "the generous public spirit which pervades Great Britain" and also declared that he now understood "more keenly than ever what a constitutional government and an enlightened people mean." His understanding of the latter consideration, he said, meant that he was now "prepared to pursue the cause of advancement, education, and civilization, in my own beloved but oppressed country." Sun also took great care to publicize his Christianity, even though he hardly ever went to church during his stay in England. (He was later to assert that he "did not belong to the Christianity of the churches, but to the Christianity of Jesus, who was a revolutionary.")

In his political pronouncements to British journalists and civic leaders, Sun studiously avoided portraying his program as containing revolutionary or republican elements. The Chinese reform movement's main concern, he said, was "to make the present system [the Manchu-Mandarin alliance] give place to one that is not corrupt." As China's leader, he declared, he would permit expansion of British commercial activity in his country and would welcome the assistance of European advisers and administrators in carrying out his projected reforms.

The British government, however, preferred to continue working with the Manchu regime. Within just weeks of Sun's release, the British Colonial Office ordered the governor of Hong Kong to "anticipate and frustrate any revolutionary attempts against the constituted authority in China." The "benevolent neutrality" that Sun wanted the British to show toward the Chinese reform movement was not to be forthcoming.

Despite the setbacks that he suffered in his dealings with the British authorities, Sun gained much

When residing with us in London, Sun wasted no moments in gaieties; he was forever at work, reading books on all subjects.
— JAMES CANTLIE
doctor and educator

from his experiences in London that would later be greatly to his advantage. He wrote a book, *Kidnapped in London*, that brought him to the attention of many modern thinkers all over the world. The circumstances of his release had greatly increased his awareness of the power of the press, and he was, as a result, to be extraordinarily successful at using publications to enhance his reputation and influence.

Sun's sojourn in London also gave him an excellent opportunity to further his education in Western social, economic, and political thought. Between December 1896 and June 1897, he spent 59 days at the British Museum, which houses one of the world's greatest libraries. The museum's reading room played host to many foreign radicals, including the German philosopher and economist Karl Marx, who did much of his research there. Sun would, later in his career, find much that he agreed with in the theories espoused by Marx, who believed that capitalism (the economic system based on private enterprise) contains within itself the seeds of its own destruction and that it must eventually be replaced by communism, the social order in which private property has been abolished and people live without social classes and subject to no authority. Sun would also come to admire Marx's most important intellectual disciple, Russian radical Vladimir Ilich Lenin, who masterminded the revolution that overthrew the Russian government in 1917, bringing socialism (a social order in which the workers own the means of production) to Russia. It is interesting to note that Lenin, too, spent many hours refining his revolutionary theories in the reading room of the British Museum early in his career.

Sun read widely in the museum, concentrating on those philosophical systems that he considered likely to provide him with ideas as to how China could be best changed. He also read about basic Western values like democracy as discussed by the 19th-century British philosopher John Stuart Mill and other major thinkers. Sun would later contend that his own political philosophy — which envisaged the parallel implementation of his "Three Principles" of socialism, nationalism, and democracy — had begun to be formulated during his hours of study in the British Museum. He had, almost certainly, learned a little about socialism while moving in missionary circles in Hong Kong, and during his stay in London, Sun had come to know of the campaign that was then being conducted by British socialists against the widespread poverty that had come to plague Britain as a result of unregulated capitalism.

In July 1897 Sun left England and embarked upon a fund-raising tour of overseas Chinese communities in Canada. He met with little success, barely raising enough money for passage to his next destination, Japan. There Sun made the acquaintance of Torazo Miyazaki, a young Japanese radical not unlike himself. Miyazaki was a proponent of pan-Asianism, an ideology whose devotees believed that Europeans would never consider Asians their equals and that Asian cooperation with Western imperialism was fundamentally wrong. The pan-Asianists believed that Japan should encourage and assist reform in China, and that the two countries should eventually unite to eliminate European colonial rule in Asia. To Miyazaki and other pan-Asianists, the idea of Japanese sponsorship and tutelage of Chinese renewal was immensely attractive.

There were also many Japanese — especially among the country's leading politicians and senior civil servants and soldiers — who were more than willing to proclaim pan-Asianism while practicing (or at least encouraging) Japanese imperialism. Some Japanese had read Sun's book *Kidnapped in London* and thought that it might be possible to exploit his radicalism to expand Japanese interests on the Asian mainland. And Miyazaki had excellent contacts in the upper levels of the Japanese bureaucracy, where the expansionist group was strongly represented.

While Sun had been furthering his education in London and gaining an understanding of pan-Asianism in Japan, momentous changes had taken place in China, changes that were to present him

EASTFOTO

The Empress Dowager Ci Xi vehemently resisted social change. Although she took her luxuries, like opium smoking, in strict moderation, she was notorious for her cruelty and violent homicidal rages.

Emilio Aguinaldo, the Philippine revolutionary leader, at first welcomed the American forces who captured his country from the Spanish in 1898. It soon became clear that the United States intended to keep the Philippines as a colony, however, and Aguinaldo, aided by Sun, began a guerrilla war against the Americans.

with new challenges and new opportunities. The young Manchu emperor, Guang Xu, had come under the influence of a group of reform-minded mandarins led by a brilliant Confucian scholar named Kang Youwei and a radical journalist named Liang Qichao. Kang hoped that China could be made into a constitutional monarchy, modeled upon the one that was then in existence in Japan. But the changes that Kang suggested and the emperor tried to implement were considered too sweeping by moderate reformers, conservative mandarins, and the military.

In September 1898 the conservatives rallied their forces around the old empress dowager, Ci Xi, who was Guang Xu's aunt and adoptive mother. Ci Xi stormed out of retirement, locked up the young emperor, and crushed the reformers. Kang and Liang barely escaped with their lives. Several other reformers were not so fortunate; the empress dowager had them executed.

These events, known as the "Hundred Days' Reform" because they had lasted about that long, greatly complicated Sun's search for supporters. Kang and Liang, who took refuge in Japan and later traveled the world promoting their own vision of reform for China, were at that time much more famous than Sun. Kang was the most celebrated Confucian scholar of the late Qing period, and Liang had a reputation as a highly learned modern scholar and journalist. Many Chinese, both at home and abroad, thought the Kang-Liang program for a constitutional monarchy more reasonable than Sun's demands for revolutionary change. While Sun wanted a republican form of government, headed by elected officials, the moderates who supported Kang and Liang were willing to retain China's most ancient institution, the imperial throne.

While working in concert with the Japanese pan-Asianists, Sun got involved in a wide variety of political activities. The first of these brought him into contact with a revolution in the Philippines.

The Philippines, which had been a colony of Spain since the 16th century, came under American control in 1898, when the United States emerged victorious from the Spanish-American War. Filipino nationalists, led by Emilio Aguinaldo, initially welcomed the American presence, thinking that the U.S. government would soon grant the Philippines independence. But by the summer of 1898, it became clear to the Filipinos that the Americans intended to stay. Aguinaldo then began a guerrilla war against them. Miyazaki met with Filipino nationalists in Hong Kong in 1898, and promised to help send arms to Aguinaldo's forces.

The Japanese supported Aguinaldo as part of their policy of minimizing foreign influence in Asia. At the same time, they did not wish to antagonize the United States, and therefore took care to conceal their involvement, working outside official channels and arranging for financing and arms purchases through adventurers like Miyazaki. Another of their tactics was to have weapons and other military equipment purchased and handled not by a Japanese, but by a Chinese: Sun Yat-sen.

Sun needed no encouragement to participate in this project and, in so doing, was more than a mere tool of the Japanese. He considered supporting the Filipino freedom fighters a great opportunity for Sino-Japanese cooperation in the fight against Western imperialism in Asia and willingly managed the negotiations for the purchase, shipment, and delivery of arms. No Japanese arms were to reach the Philippines, however. The first munitions ship dispatched by Sun and his associates sank in a storm, and their plans for a second shipment had to be abandoned when the Japanese government, informed that U.S. military intelligence had discovered what was going on, ordered the project to be discontinued. Aguinaldo, whose forces were eventually defeated by U.S. troops in 1902, sent Sun a considerable amount of money as a mark of his appreciation of Sun's efforts. The Philippine leader's generosity enabled Sun to finance his first revolutionary publication, a newspaper called the *China Mail*, which was circulated among the overseas Chinese and focused on delivering sustained criticism of the Kang-Liang reform program.

The fact that Sun greatly admired American de-

This 1899 cartoon shows Emilio Aguinaldo crushed by American might. The Japanese offered covert aid to the Philippine freedom fighters through an agent, Sun Yatsen, who considered this project an opportunity to rid Asia of foreign intervention and influence.

> *The real trouble is that China is not an independent country. She is the victim of foreign countries.*
>
> —SUN YAT-SEN

mocracy and was fascinated by the strength and complexity of the American economy has frequently led people to ask why he was so willing to cooperate with the Japanese against American interests. This question can best be answered if one remembers that anti-imperialism was the dominant concept in Asian politics at the time. Chinese and Japanese all agreed that additional Western influence in Asia, and particularly the establishment of new colonies, was to be prevented if at all possible. While the primary concern of the Chinese revolutionaries was the backwardness of their own government, the ever-increasing threat of expanded foreign domination was also of vital importance.

In collaborating with the Japanese, Sun was, on some levels at least, working against the long-term interests of his country. Japan had already taken control of Taiwan province and, as the expansionist faction within her ruling circles came to dominate Japanese politics, would eventually seek to secure absolute control of China's northern provinces. The Japanese wanted to increase their power and influence in China, and Sun was surely aware of their motives.

It must be understood that Sun's frequent willingness to work with rapacious foreigners in order to enhance his own influence and to further the cause to which he had dedicated his life in no way detracts from his stature as China's first great revolutionary. In fact, this aspect of his approach to revolutionary politics marks him as a masterful tactician. Circumstances often forced Sun to forge alliances that were to his immediate advantage but whose long-term implications were disastrous. However, it was always to be the case that prospective disasters never became reality. Sun's tactical skills, which were always fortified by his seemingly inexhaustible self-assurance, invariably enabled him to maintain a sense of perspective and direction in even the most volatile situations. These skills were to be tested yet again in 1900, when Sun and his colleagues attempted to take advantage of the situation that had developed in China following the conclusion of the Sino-Japanese War.

The massive reparations that the Japanese had demanded of China under the terms of the Treaty of Shimonoseki quickly turned China into a debtor nation. The country's capital reserves were insufficiently substantial to allow for disbursements on the scale contemplated by the Japanese, and the Chinese government was forced to seek assistance from foreign bankers. The foreign loans were duly forthcoming, but only on terms that were highly disadvantageous to the Chinese. The Western banks charged outlandishly high rates of interest and insisted that the loans, which were linked to the price of gold on the world financial markets, be secured against Chinese government revenues. As a result, by 1899 China's foreign debt was three times greater than the government's annual income, and the country's tax system was operating for the benefit of foreign investors.

As the country's economic condition deteriorated, the Chinese people became increasingly restive. They were now finding it harder than ever simply to survive, did not understand why, and consequently sought to vent their frustration and anger. A major crisis was developing, and its eruption was to encourage Sun and his supporters to resume revolutionary activity on the Chinese mainland.

A Japanese lithograph shows Japanese troops marching into a Taiwanese village in 1895 after the Sino-Japanese War. Although the Japanese had gained control of Taiwan and were hoping to move into China's northern provinces, Sun continued to cooperate with them in order to expand his own political influence.

4

In Search of Victory

In 1899 political developments in northern China became the focus of international attention. A previously obscure secret society called the Boxers (so named because they were devotees of the traditional Chinese martial art of boxing) began conducting a campaign of terror against foreigners, quickly attracting the support of thousands of peasants. The Boxers, most of whom were extremely poor and very young, believed that by practicing boxing they could become invulnerable to bullets. The widespread antiforeign incidents and uprisings that were inspired by their insurgency rapidly became known as the Boxer Rebellion.

The immediate cause of the Boxer Rebellion was severe flooding in the north, which left millions of peasants in Shandong province both homeless and, when government relief efforts proved inadequate, thoroughly disaffected. The situation was rendered even more explosive by popular hostility toward the German presence in the area. German soldiers, prospectors, and merchants had consistently treated the Chinese with contempt, and any protests made by the victims of their prejudice were crushed with singular brutality. The German emperor himself, Wilhelm II, had earlier declared that "hundreds of thousands of Chinese will quiver when they feel the iron fist of Germany on their necks."

There was that inexplicable something about him that stamped him as a leader of men.
—GEORGE LYNCH
American writer,
on Sun Yat-sen

Imprisoned members of the Chinese secret society called the Boxers. The Boxer Rebellion in 1899 attracted international attention and caused internal alarm as thousands of young peasants rampaged through northern China, killing many missionaries and Christian Chinese.

THE BETTMANN ARCHIVE

UPI/BETTMANN NEWSPHOTOS

During the Boxer Rebellion, missionaries were executed and their bodies thrown into a pit. The peasants who participated in the Huizhou uprising, however, impressed both Sun and foreign observers with their discipline and restraint, as no missionary stations were attacked and no villages were looted.

Our Empire is now laboring under great difficulties which are becoming daily more serious. The various powers cast upon us looks of tiger-like voracity, hustling each other in their endeavors to be the first to seize upon our innermost territories.

— CI XI
Chinese empress, from a message to her viceroys sent during the Boxer Rebellion

Shandong was not, however, the only hotbed of discontent in China. The economy was becoming increasingly depressed, in part because cheap foreign imports were destroying China's traditional craft-based industries and also because national indebtedness to foreign bankers had forced the government to raise taxes. The latter development was particularly important, since most of China's peasants were in no position to shoulder the increased tax burden.

In early 1899, the Boxers began striking out at the most visible signs of the foreign presence in China: the missionary establishments. In the countryside, some 250 foreigners, mostly missionaries, were killed by angry mobs, and many more Chinese Christians also died at Boxer hands. Expelled from Shandong in the middle of 1899 by Yuan Shikai — the provincial governor who thought the Boxer insurgency likely to provoke a major Western military intervention — the Boxers then went on the rampage in the metropolitan province of Chihli. There, the Boxers discovered that the authorities were prepared to sanction their activities. This official approval was mainly due to developments at court, where the empress dowager and her antireformist conservative advisers were by no means averse to the advent of a popular uprising that was not aimed at the ruling dynasty. By the end of 1899, imperial support for the boxers was manifest, and the Boxer war cry had become "Support the Qing, exterminate the foreigners."

In May 1900 the foreign powers decided to take precautionary action, sending a force of 400 troops to protect the legation quarter in Beijing, where the foreign embassies and residences were concentrated. On June 10 another foreign relief force, numbering 2,000 men, left Tianjin for Beijing. Pro-Boxer elements took advantage of this latest development to persuade the empress dowager that the foreigners intended to remove her from power and restore the young emperor to the throne. On June 18 the relief forces were repulsed by imperial troops and fell back on Tianjin. Tensions finally came to a head on June 20, when, following the assassination of the German ambassador by a Chinese soldier, the Boxers began a siege of the legation quarter. On June 21, 1900, the pro-Boxer government in Beijing declared war on the foreign powers.

American troops marching in front of a Beijing temple. The Western powers consolidated forces and battled the Boxers during the spring and summer of 1900.

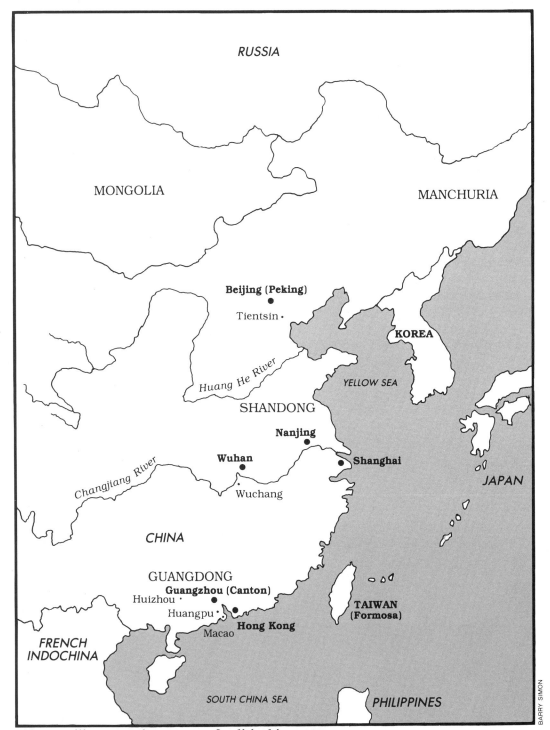

This map illustrates those areas of political importance in eastern Asia during Sun's lifetime, a period of turbulent transition for China. After the 1911 Revolution, when the imperial government finally collapsed, China would undergo nearly another 40 years of political, social, and economic upheaval.

In July the foreign powers put together another expedition and fought through to Beijing to lift the month-long siege of the legation quarter. Although the foreign powers won the war with the Boxers, the Chinese government forces fought better than they ever had before. The fighting was, however, almost entirely restricted to the north, since the governors of the central and southern provinces, taking a more realistic view of the situation, refused to participate in the conflict. Many of them claimed that the declaration of war had been the work of "rebels who had usurped power in Beijing."

The Boxer Rebellion was a turning point in Chinese history. Even the Manchus and the conservative mandarins who supported them saw that unless they instituted major reforms they would fall, either before the foreign powers or at the hands of their own people. The foreigners, for their part, now realized that the days of easy victories in China were over. They would have to depend more on diplomacy and less on military might. For the revolutionaries, the Boxer Rebellion and the subsequent political isolation of the ruling elite indicated that imperial China was in her death throes and that action taken now could prove decisive.

It was in this atmosphere of heightened crisis that Sun and his colleagues began planning another rising. The revolutionaries designated Huizhou, in Guangdong, as their theater of operations, and anticipated launching the rebellion in the late fall of 1900. Huizhou, which was already suffering widespread civil unrest, was a haven for bandits, pirates, and smugglers, many of whom were recruited by Sun's lieutenants. For most of the period during which plans for the uprising were being made, Sun was in Taiwan negotiating for support from the island province's new Japanese administration, many of whose members were more willing to get involved in Sun's venture (which they hoped to exploit for expansionist purposes) than their more cautious colleagues in Tokyo, the Japanese capital.

Unfortunately for Sun and his associates, the British police in Hong Kong (where the revolutionaries had concentrated their fund-raising and logistical efforts) got wind of the conspiracy and began to make life difficult for them. The situation was made even more critical by the fact that Sun had been unable to secure sufficient munitions for his striking force of 600 men, which had been in place and waiting for orders in Huizhou for several weeks. By the end of September most of the men had returned to their homes. Those who remained found themselves facing encirclement by thousands of government troops.

Fighting broke out between government troops and what was left of the rebel strike force on October 6, 1900. Sun had sent a message ordering his men to disperse earlier that same day, but by the time it arrived a detachment of 80 rebels had beaten a superior government force and was already attracting peasant recruits. On October 7 the Japanese expansionists in Taiwan finally offered to send Sun's forces weapons, and possibly a number of military advisers, if the rebels could secure Amoy (in Fujian province), the southern Chinese port closest to Taiwan. Sun immediately ordered his forces not to march on Guangzhou (which had been their original target) and to make for Amoy instead.

During the next two weeks, hordes of peasants and defectors from the imperial army joined the rebel forces, which eventually numbered around 10,000 men. Since only 2,000 of them had rifles, however, they were unable to maintain the offensive for very long. On October 20 a government force of 20,000 troops checked the rebel advance 150 miles west of Amoy. The campaign came to an abrupt end, on Sun's orders, three days later, when the Japanese expansionists in Taiwan informed Sun that they had received orders from Tokyo forbidding them to assist the Chinese rebels. Sun's disappointment at this announcement became even greater when he then decided to make use of the weapons he had been unable to ship to Aguinaldo only to discover that they did not exist. His Japanese agent had stolen the money with which they had supposedly been purchased.

Sun's disappointment at the failure of the Huizhou uprising was tempered by his realization that during its course he had learned much that would be of assistance in the future. The rising had revealed that China's peasants would support an antidynastic movement. It was now apparent that they were capable of venting their frustration against the government that had capitulated to foreign interests rather than against the representatives of those interests. The discipline that the peasants displayed during the rising had greatly impressed not only Sun and his lieutenants but many foreign observers. The peasants attacked no missionary establishments and looted no villages for supplies, generally behaving with a restraint that was nowhere in evidence among the government forces. The peasants' responsiveness to the revolutionaries' aims convinced Sun that he had perhaps found a valuable — and, ultimately, overwhelmingly powerful—new constituency.

In evaluating the Huizhou rising, Sun also came to the conclusion that Japan had become an unreliable ally. He felt that his Japanese supporters' failure to deliver on their promises had cost him both victory and the lives of many brave men. Accordingly, he turned to another foreign power for support.

In late 1902 Sun received an invitation from the French ambassador in Tokyo to visit Saigon and Hanoi, the two most important cities in France's Indochinese colonies, which included Laos, Cambodia, Tonkin, Annam, and Cochin China. Sun accepted the invitation and, after meeting with sympathizers in Hong Kong en route, arrived in Hanoi in December 1902.

The ambassador's invitation marked the beginning of a long and important relationship between Sun and French expansionists in Vietnam and in France. After ascertaining that the French would indeed assist him in the revolutionary operations that he proposed to conduct across the frontier in southern China, Sun decided to tour the United States to recruit supporters and raise money.

Sun went first to Hawaii, in the fall of 1903, and stayed with his family for six months while making arrangements to tour the continental United States.

Sun viewed the "overseas Chinese" communities in Europe and the United States as a viable source of financial support for the revolutionary movement in China. Here, during the Chinese New Year in Los Angeles, California, celebrants watch as Tsewje, the lion, battles "evil spirits."

The political activist Huang Xing helped Sun organize the Chinese United League in 1905. Sun was convinced that members of the new generation of radical Chinese — such as Huang Xing — would become an integral part of the revolution.

XINHUA NEWS AGENCY

He was well received by the overseas Chinese community in Hawaii, many of whom, having observed the repeated failures of the Manchu regime, were now more sympathetic to the idea of revolution than they had ever been before.

From April to August of 1904, Sun toured the United States with Huang Sande, one of the most prominent secret society leaders in that country. Sun spoke at lodges in Sacramento, Fresno, and Colusa, California. Despite the fact that his reputation had risen considerably since his previous tour, his reception in many of the communities he visited was lukewarm. The Chinese-American communities were somewhat conservative, and many supported the moderate reformism espoused by Kang Youwei. Sun and Huang Sande tried for six months to raise money and recruit supporters, but were eventually forced to cut their tour short. At the end of the year, Sun left for Europe to reestablish his ties with foreign supporters there and to work with Chinese students.

The Chinese government's decision to start sending students to Europe as part of the cautious reform program it had initiated in the wake of the Boxer Rebellion had as much to do with the containment of revolution as it did with securing Western educations for the country's best intellects. Many of the students were political militants whom the government wanted as far away from China as possible. Sun found the majority of the students with whom he met amenable to his ideas about nationalism, democracy, and socialism. His audiences were less impressed, however, with the fact that he considered the secret societies a vital base of revolutionary power. The students felt that the predominantly lower-class secret society members lacked political sophistication and could not, therefore, reasonably be expected to constitute an effective revolutionary vanguard. Sun eventually conceded that intellectuals could indeed make an important — perhaps decisive — contribution to the revolutionary project and, as a result, secured the allegiance of a group of extremely militant students from Hubei province. Those same students also recommended Sun to their friends among the Chinese student community in Tokyo.

In June 1905 Sun left Europe for Japan. He stopped over at Saigon, in Cochin China, where he further developed his ties with the French authorities and the overseas Chinese radicals in the region. When he arrived in Japan, he found that support

I have heard Dr. Sun Yat-sen addressing a meeting of his countrymen. His listeners never tired of listening to him.
— J. ELLIS BARKER
writer

Sun headed a well-organized student movement comprised of young and eager leaders like Qiu Jin, a political activist from Zhejiang province. Her anti-Manchu militias staged an armed uprising in 1907.

for revolution had increased markedly among the 13,000 Chinese students then resident in that country.

Many of the students were political refugees, one of whom, a remarkable man named Huang Xing, became Sun's comrade in arms. Huang Xing was an energetic political activist and a leading member of the Changjiang Valley secret society known as the "Society of Brothers and Elders." Huang had been involved in an abortive uprising in 1904 in Changsha, a city in Hunan province.

When Sun returned to Japan, Huang Xing, urged on by the Japanese expansionists, proposed that his own group and Sun's should combine forces. Sun, whose European tour had convinced him that the new generation of radical Chinese students would be invaluable to the revolutionary cause, thought the idea a good one. The new organization, which was founded on August 20, 1905, was called the Zhongguo Tong Meng Hui, often translated as the "Chinese United League." The organization's members were required to make vows of loyalty to Sun's four aims — "expulsion of the Manchus, restoration of Chinese rule, the establishment of a republic, and equalization of land rights." Sun was elected president of the organization, and Huang Xing became his deputy. The Chinese United League also established a newspaper, the *Min Bao*, or *People's Journal*. First published in February 1906, the *People's Journal* became a major vehicle for the dissemination of Sun's ideas and served further to enhance his reputation.

Within two years the Chinese United League had 900 members, most of whom joined in Japan. Although the new group was composed mainly of students, Sun made it clear that its activities in China were to be carried on primarily through the secret societies. It was a large and diverse group, and not always easy to control. Many of its more militant members allowed their eagerness for action to take precedence over routine political work, often initiating risings without consulting the organization's leaders. Sometimes the student radical groups used the name of the Chinese United League, and sometimes they did not. One leader of such a group was the activist and educator Qiu Jin, who helped organize a training center for anti-Manchu militias. Qiu also politicized the curriculum at the girls' school at which she was teaching and used it as a center for an armed rising in 1907. The rising failed due to poor communications, however, and Qiu Jin was executed.

In February 1907 the Chinese government, angered by the success with which Sun had met in circulating his ideas and consolidating his leadership of the Chinese United League, made formal protests to the Japanese government for harboring him. Their representations came at a time when Sun's Japanese supporters had lost much of their previous influence in official circles. Having fought and won a war with Russia for commercial supremacy in Manchuria and political supremacy in Korea in 1905, Japan was now an imperial power in its own right and equally as determined to extract concessions from the Chinese government as any European nation. Cultivating the support of Chinese revolutionaries — whose socialist inclinations had always been anathema to Japan's ruling circles — had ceased to be an instrument of policy, and even the most ardent Japanese expansionists considered the consolidation of Japan's existing overseas interests in northeastern China more important than attempting to secure a foothold in southern China, where Sun's supporters were concentrated. His pan-Asianist Japanese allies were unable to protect him, and in March Sun was expelled from Japan.

Despite this disappointing turn of events, Sun was now at a high point in his career. He had won over hundreds of radical students and also forged a working relationship with the overseas Chinese in Indochina. He still had the backing of principled Japanese pan-Asianists like Torazo Miyazaki and had gained a brave and determined new comrade in Huang Xing. Such were the advantages that Sun enjoyed when he and his entourage left Japan for Hanoi to plan armed uprisings across the border in southern China.

> *If Sun Yat-sen had one consistent talent, it was for failure. Yet he remains a national hero because the more than quarter of a century in which he was active was the darkest period of modern Chinese history, and without his memory it would seem even darker.*
> —HAROLD Z. SCHIFFRIN
> Israeli historian

5

The Mounting Flames of Revolution

Sun had many reasons for selecting the Sino-Indochinese border area as his next battlefield. The adjacent southern Chinese provinces of Guangxi and Guangdong had been prone to outbreaks of civil unrest ever since the Taiping Rebellion. The majority of the population lived in extreme poverty and had little affection for the government, whose control of the region was tenuous at best. Mountainous terrain provided perfect sanctuary for rebels, and the many secret societies in the area would need very little encouragement to stage uprisings.

The French colonial authorities viewed Sun in much the same light as had the Japanese. Some of Sun's supporters in Indochina and in France were, like his Japanese connections, closely allied with industrial and commercial interests. Sun accordingly promised them substantial influence and opportunities if he were successful. At the same time, as had also been the case with regard to Japan, there were competing French interests that considering it more prudent to protect the advantages France had already secured, fully supported the Manchu regime.

Dr. Sun likens the vast provinces of the Chinese empire to the state of the American Union, needing only a president to govern all alike.
—the *Pacific Commercial Advertiser,* a Honolulu newspaper

Sun moved his revolutionary operations to southern China in 1907. Sun's attacks on the Manchu government were at first unsuccessful, but by 1911 the tottering Qing dynasty was ready to fall.

With French help, Sun made contact with the lawless adventurers—known as "Roving Braves"—who inhabited the border area. The Roving Braves, who were bandits, supported themselves mainly by smuggling opium from China to Indochina, where its price was kept very high by the French administration, which sold it under official monopoly to help defray the costs of the colony. Having quickly discovered that the Roving Braves' political awareness was as insignificant as their fighting abilities were legendary, Sun enlisted them as mercenaries through his secret society contacts in Hanoi and Saigon. The leaders of two of the largest and most active groups of Roving Braves operating across the border in south China, Wang Heixun, and Huang Mingdang, were selected to lead the risings.

Sun's first opportunity came when a peasant revolt erupted protesting increased taxation in the border county of Jinzhou, in Guangdong province. Wang Heixun led an attack on Fangzheng, the county seat, on September 1, 1907. But the Roving Braves, like most mercenaries, proved undependable, often refusing to fight unless the odds were overwhelmingly in their favor, which they rarely were. Their leaders were more interested in displacing each other than they were in overthrowing the Manchus, and the revolt sputtered and died.

In analyzing this defeat, Sun came to the conclusion that one shortcoming of the strategy of fomenting uprisings in trouble spots like Jinzhou was that such isolated incidents permitted the Manchu forces to concentrate until they had achieved decisive numerical superiority over the rebels. Sun accordingly developed an ambitious new plan, whereby coordinated attacks would be launched along three adjoining border passes between Tonkin and Guangxi province.

Sun believed that Guangxi's numerous anti-Manchu organizations would rally to his cause if he could assure them a sufficiency of weapons and supplies. The creation of a revolutionary base in the region would therefore depend upon whether or not he could secure French assistance and approval for his plan to send arms and supplies into China by

rail from Tonkin. The project was further complicated by the fact that Sun's mercenaries — whose
unreliability also represented a major threat to his
chances of success — would be advancing through
difficult terrain.

In planning this ambitious three-pronged assault, Sun soon encountered some familiar problems. The disparate elements of his forces would
not cooperate, and money and munitions were in
short supply. Finally, Sun decided to attack only the
most important of the three passes, Zhennanguan.

On December 1, 1907, Huang Mingdang attacked
the fortress that guarded the pass. Because many
of the Chinese soldiers had already agreed to join
the rebels or, failing that, desert their posts, resistance was light. Once the forts had been secured,
the rebels sent word to Sun, who was directing the
operation from Hanoi. Accompanied by Huang
Xing, some local anti-Manchu leaders, and a French
artilleryman, Sun hiked into the pass, linking up
with his forces on the night of December 3. It was
the first time Sun had been on Chinese soil since
1900.

**The smoking of opium be-
came popular in China as il-
licit trading of the drug by
the British East India Company flourished during the
1780s. In the early 1900s
opium was smuggled be-
tween China and French
Indochina.**

Execution of a Chinese criminal. Beheading was a popular method of execution in China right into the 20th century, as political factions battled each other to gain control of China.

As dawn began to break, the rebels found that their situation was far from promising. They hoped to capture considerable amounts of weapons and ammunition but found only a few outmoded muskets. The modern, German-manufactured field guns that constituted the fort's main armament had been disabled, and the French artilleryman, who had been brought along for just this purpose, was able to repair only one of them. The gun was then fired at a nearby government-held fortification, inflicting several casualties.

Recognizing that possession of a single field gun would hardly suffice to give his forces a decisive advantage, Sun decided that the situation demanded emergency measures. He immediately returned to Hanoi, intending to procure money and arms from his French supporters. His negotiations with French financiers, which proved futile, came to an abrupt end when he was informed that the Manchu forces had regrouped and recaptured the forts and Zhennanguan.

Although the border risings had failed, they were ultimately of great benefit to Sun in that they served to increase his fame both throughout Indochina and in his homeland. That such notoriety also had its drawbacks became apparent when the French colonial authorities in Indochina began to receive requests from the Chinese government that Sun be expelled. Finally, in January 1908, alarmed by the pressure from both Beijing and Paris and disturbed by the fact that the Chinese rebels' revolutionary ideas had begun to infect many of his own colonial subjects, French Governor-general Paul Beau had Sun deported from Indochina.

During the next two months, Sun, now based in Singapore, made plans for another attack in Jinzhou, where local anti-Manchu elements were continuing to foment unrest. Huang Xing, who was to lead the assault, organized two units, one composed of Roving Braves, the other of overseas Chinese from Indochina.

On March 27, 1908, Huang's forces crossed the border from Tonkin into China. The invaders moved at will throughout their target area until the end of April, when the number of government forces in the area made further action inadvisable. The pattern that had emerged during previous uprisings was repeated: the peasants returned to their homes, supplies and munitions ran low, and internal disputes damaged the cohesion of the rebel forces. Yet another uprising had ended in failure.

This operation, like the earlier ones, had originally been planned as one element of coordinated regional uprising. The other area selected as a center of revolutionary activity was on the Tonkin border with Yunnan province, at the Hekou Pass. Yunnan was of particular interest to a French railroad firm, the Société de Construction des Chemins de Fer du Yunnan, whose directors were prepared to support Sun's organization in order to secure a railhead in Yunnan. Such a facility would give their company an outstanding advantage in trade with southern China.

After he left the failed uprising in Jinzhou, Huang Xing moved on to Hekou, where the insurrection

planned for that area was now under way. Led by
Huang Mingdang, Roving Braves and defectors from
the Chinese army had seized the border forts and
were waiting for support from Sun's group. Huang
Xing arrived at the scene and tried to persuade the
Roving Braves to push on up the railroad and take
the closest Chinese city, Mengci, whose massive ar-
senal would provide sufficient weapons to arm all
who had rallied to the rebel cause.

The continuing failure of the revolutionary forces
to advance into Yunnan began to alarm the French,
who now doubted that Sun's armies were capable
of winning. To the French, the rebels seemed as
disorganized as the government forces. When the
French then decided that they would give the revolutionaries no assistance unless they took Mengci,
Sun found himself confronted with one of the most
critical situations of his career. His forces were on
the verge of seizing a large part of Yunnan, securing
adequate arms and receiving immediate and substantial aid from French railroad and banking interests. Huang Xing had to capture Mengci.

Using every inducement from coercion to bribery,
Huang Xing made repeated efforts to get Huang
Mingdang to advance. Finally, abandoning all hope
of getting what he wanted out of Huang Mingdang,
Huang Xing took charge of a group of 100 Roving
Braves himself and managed to get them marching.
Only minutes into the march, however, the Roving
Braves came to a halt, sat down, and refused to go
any further. When the increasingly desperate
Huang Xing ordered them forward, they fired their
rifles into the air. Realizing that he could no longer
control the mercenaries, Huang Xing left for Hanoi,
intending to bring up a unit of loyal overseas
Chinese. When he tried to get back into Tonkin,
however, he was mistaken for a Japanese spy by the
French border police, who arrested him.

The uprising, which had begun so promisingly,
thus ended in defeat. The rebels continued to operate until the end of May, when, once again, government forces reestablished their supremacy in
the region. The situation became even worse when
what little confidence Sun's French supporters still

had in him was destroyed due to excesses committed by the mercenaries he had hired.

While the Roving Braves were retreating from Hekou, a group of them was captured in Tonkin by French-led Indochinese soldiers. That night, another group of Roving Braves fired into the French camp and killed two French officers, two sergeants, and a number of Indochinese soldiers. The victims' bodies were then decapitated and mutilated. The French community in Indochina was outraged and immediately offered a bounty for every Chinese head brought in by local tribesmen. The French also deported more than 600 of Sun's men to Singapore.

By 1908 Sun had reached the low point of his career. He had been expelled first from Japan and then from Indochina. In Japan, the Chinese United League was divided by internal disputes, and the *People's Journal* had been suspended by the Japanese government. Some revolutionaries were questioning Sun's honesty and accusing him of diverting funds, and foreign support for the revolutionary cause had all but evaporated. Regaining the initiative might have seemed impossible to a less determined man than Sun at this point, and he could easily have chosen to live out his life in comfort with his family in Hawaii. But his fierce determination to free his beloved country from the decadent Manchus was undiminished, and he decided to survey his old contacts and see what could be done.

In May 1909 Sun left Singapore and traveled to Europe. His efforts to secure assistance from banking and commercial interests in London and Paris were unsuccessful, and he therefore turned once again to the United States. In December 1909 Sun arrived in San Francisco, where he persuaded the secret society leader Huang Sande to accompany him on a fund-raising tour of southern California. During the tour, he discovered that his reputation among the Chinese-American communities had improved substantially. He also became acutely aware of the fact that the combined life savings of a few hundred Chinese laundrymen could hardly be expected to finance a revolution. His spirits began to

The Tomb of the 72 Martyrs in Guangzhou is dedicated to the members of the Chinese United League who died in the April 1911 uprising. The Guangzhou rebellion failed after army units that had agreed to support Sun's group refused to mutiny.

XINHUA NEWS AGENCY

Sun in elaborate military costume. Though his role in the revolutionary movement was essentially administrative, Sun did participate in overall military strategy.

rise again, however, when he was informed that lieutenants in Hong Kong had been contacted by dissident Chinese soldiers in Guangdong, who asked for the revolutionaries' assistance in planning an uprising. Their subsequent action, which became known as the Guangdong New Army Revolt of 1910, encountered many of the difficulties that usually faced rebel groups. Because of government countermeasures, the mutineers were forced to commence operations ahead of schedule, and some of the groups that had promised to participate backed out. Coordination between the units that did participate was inadequate, and the several thousand troops who mutinied were bloodily suppressed.

To Sun and his colleagues, the involvement of disaffected government troops in an anti-Manchu uprising indicated that opposition to the dynasty was finally beginning to erode the very foundation of the Manchu state. The pace of change was undoubtedly accelerating, but the prospect of victory remained distant. His group began planning yet another uprising. This one was to be different from previous ventures in that it would be methodically planned and would rely not upon the secret societies, but upon trained, trusted, and politically sophisticated cadres who would move into the Guangzhou area to supervise the entire operation. Since such an ambitious effort would clearly require substantial funding, Sun, who had been staying in Japan and Singapore, himself returned to Europe and North America to raise the money.

While Sun was meeting with secret society lodges in Canada, the situation in Guangzhou unexpectedly deteriorated. On April 8, 1911, five days before the insurrection was due to commence, an overeager revolutionary assassinated a key Manchu military official, thus alerting the authorities. As a result, the Chinese army units that had pledged to support the rebels refused to mutiny. Finally, Huang Xing, who had been put in charge of the uprising, became convinced that unless he acted immediately the whole operation would fail. The main revolutionary force duly conducted a series of assaults on government installations, but, having lost the element of surprise, encountered heavy opposition and was forced to retreat.

Despite the failure of the rising, Sun was now convinced that his optimism concerning the prospects for substantial revolutionary gains in China was entirely justified. Mutinies, uprisings, and assassinations of government officials were becoming routine events in many parts of the country.

During the summer of 1911, two Changjiang Valley revolutionary groups that had little contact with Sun's Chinese United League began to plan a major uprising. The "Common Advancement Society" and the "Literary Society" (so named to avoid arousing official suspicion) had little interest in republicanism but were determined to bring down the Manchu dynasty. Both organizations had enrolled thousands of Chinese soldiers and enjoyed something of a practical advantage over Sun's group in that their leaders were not preoccupied with drumming up foreign support and funding. In September 1911 the two organizations agreed to combine forces and scheduled the uprising for mid-October. Although they were forced to move ahead of the designated time when one of their munitions stores exploded on October 9, the rebels nevertheless managed to retain the initiative. By October 12 they had cap-

Members of a Chinese bomb corps display their hand-grenade-throwing technique. Sun was in London when word reached him that the revolution had erupted and the Manchu dynasty was about to fall.

THE BETTMANN ARCHIVE

Yuan Shikai, first president of the Chinese Republic. Although the British supported the choice of Yuan Shikai for president, Sun was the over-whelming choice of the Chinese people. Hoping to avoid further disunity in his country, Sun graciously stepped aside for Yuan.

tured the industrial center of Wuhan. During the next two months, most Chinese provinces — including all the provinces of southern China — declared for the revolution. It was at this point in China's crisis that Yuan Shikai came to the forefront of events as the leader of China's most modern armies (the main support of the failing Manchu regime) and managed to secure the allegiance of most of the provinces in the north of the country. The revolutionary movements in the south (most of which were republican-oriented) thus found themselves forced to maneuver within a revolution that was partly of their making but in many respects not entirely to their liking.

Sun, who was in the United States at this time, read in the American press that he was being proposed for the presidency of a future Chinese republic in many quarters. He did not, however, return to China immediately. Recognizing that the success of the infant revolution and the security of his own position would hinge upon the attitudes of the foreign powers, Sun decided to attempt to appeal directly to the governments of the United States, Britain, and France. His primary objective was to secure foreign approval of his program and proof of that approval in the form of foreign loans. Sun realized that if the foreign powers should choose to make additional loans to the Qing dynasty (which was now virtually bankrupt) to protect their acquired rights and their investments, then the regime might fight on. But if the foreign powers were to recognize the revolutionaries, then the rebels would themselves be eligible for foreign loans and the success of the revolution would loom much closer.

By the time Sun arrived in London at the end of October, the British government had already decided it wished to see Yuan Shikai come to power. Yuan, whom the foreign powers considered suitably conservative and very much more of a known quantity than Sun, was already consulting closely with the British ambassador in Beijing, Sir John Jordan. The British also knew that they could not afford to show unqualified support for Yuan, since doing so might provoke antiforeign incidents in the rebel-held south. Another factor that entered into the British government's calculations was the extent of Sun's influence and popularity among the Chinese residents of Britain's prized Asian colonies, Hong Kong and Singapore.

Having failed to secure a commitment of support from the British, Sun traveled to Paris. His negotiations with French bankers and politicians proved fruitless, and it was becoming increasingly apparent that the foreign powers were all lining up behind Yuan Shikai. The Japanese, who had acquired numerous concessions throughout northern China during the previous six years and thought Yuan's ascendancy a better guarantee of their perpetuation, now viewed Sun and his followers as dangerously radical. Japan's leaders considered the popular republic envisioned by the revolutionaries an unsuitable example for the Japanese people, many of whom favored a more democratic form of government than their own constitutional monarchy. Yuan Shikai had, in fact, assured the Japanese that he favored an interim period of constitutional monarchy, perhaps under a Manchu figurehead, followed by the establishment of a new imperial dynasty with himself as emperor.

While Yuan continued to negotiate with the foreign powers, winning them over one by one, Sun was on his way back to China. Delegates from every province in the country were meeting in Wuhan to decide who should lead the provisional government, and Sun intended to be their first choice.

6

A First Taste of Power

Sun disembarked at Shanghai on December 25, 1911, and made for Nanjing, where the leadership election was scheduled to take place on December 29. His arrival in Nanjing had a decisive effect on the provincial delegates, who had been gathered there since mid-December, furiously debating the relative merits of the leading contenders for the presidency. Sun was elected by 16 votes to 1, the single dissenting vote being cast for Huang Xing. On January 1, 1912, Sun Yat-sen was inaugurated provisional president of the Chinese Republic.

Sun was elected because, above all, he had endured. There were many other revolutionary leaders, but only Sun had been fighting for so long, since his first failed coup attempt at Guangzhou in 1898. He also had the support of thousands of overseas Chinese, many of whom had flooded Nanjing with telegrams urging his election. And he knew the world beyond China's borders better than any of his rivals.

Sun recognized, however, that Yuan Shikai would possess an overwhelming advantage in any future struggle for power. He controlled the armies of the northern provinces and also had many comrades among the southern rebels, who were disorganized and poorly supplied and lacked Yuan's access to foreign loans.

Now that the revolution is a reality, we naturally desire to see China excel the West and build up the newest and most progressive state in the world.
—SUN YAT-SEN

Sun with his second wife, Soong Ching-ling, during a journey to Beijing in 1924. They were married in 1915.

XINHUA NEWS AGENCY

When the Manchus gave up the throne in February 1912, Yuan Shikai became the president of China and the capital remained in Beijing. His leadership was highly undemocratic — in fact, he resorted to brutal methods to suppress his opponents.

Having evaluated his options, Sun came to the painful conclusion that the southern revolutionaries would have to come to terms with Yuan. They were in no position even to contemplate removing him from the political equation by force, and a civil war would be catastrophic, inviting foreign intervention. Sun chose, therefore, to subordinate all considerations of personal power and prestige to those of China's security and stability. He offered Yuan Shikai a compromise: if the Manchus would abdicate in favor of the provisional government then he would resign the presidency in favor of Yuan Shikai. This would make Yuan the leader of a united, republican China; civil war, and possible foreign intervention, would be averted.

This decision was undoubtedly painful for Sun, who had immense confidence in his abilities as a leader and had devoted his life to the pursuit of revolution and the creation of a Chinese republic. He did not trust Yuan, but, at the same time, he felt he had no alternative. Sun also felt that it might be possible to control the wily general under a representative form of government.

Yuan, and the Manchus, accepted Sun's offer, and the emperor abdicated on February 12, 1912. Imperial China had given way to the Chinese Republic. Sun Yat-sen then resigned in Nanjing, and Yuan was elected to succeed him. The generosity and selflessness that Sun had demonstrated by resigning in favor of Yuan so that the country might remain united and at peace won the hearts of the Chinese people and impressed even the most cynical foreign observers. A few months later, in August, Sun took what many thought a minor post in the new government, as director of national railroad planning. In this position, he was able to put to use his firsthand knowledge of the superior communications systems of Europe and the United States. Convinced that rail transportation would be vital to China's economic success, he traveled throughout the country lecturing on his ideas for the development of China's infrastructure. During this period, he also wrote another book, *The International Development of China*.

Sun was not able to stand aside from politics for very long. In the summer of 1912 the old Chinese United League became the Guomindang, or Nationalist party, and, as the largest political party in the new republic, dominated the country's legislative body, the National Assembly. The Guomindang was led by the brilliant Song Jiaoren, who had founded the Changjiang Valley branch of the Chinese United League.

Yuan and the National Assembly were soon locked in a struggle for supremacy. The issue at stake was whether Yuan or the elected members of the National Assembly would control the new republic. The question received a partial — and brutally direct — answer in March 1913, when Song Jiaoren, who had made it plain that he intended to use the National Assembly to make sure that Yuan could not exceed his constitutional power, was shot by a hired assassin while talking with Huang Xing in the railroad station in Shanghai. Everybody was sure that Yuan had planned the killing.

Sun presiding over the first Chinese parliament in 1912. He soon relinquished the presidency to Yuan Shikai so that China could remain peaceful and united, accepting instead a minor position in the new government as director of the railroads.

Nanjing Road, Shanghai. In 1912 the Chinese United League became the Guomindang, or Nationalist party, led by Song Jiaoren, whose group posed a threat to Yuan Shikai's authority. Later, Song Jiaoren was shot dead in a railroad station in Shanghai; many suspected the murder was the work of Yuan Shikai's forces.

Song's murder did not deter his colleagues in the Guomindang from continuing to oppose Yuan in the National Assembly. Sun, who had tried without success to persuade his political allies to declare open war against Yuan, eventually came to the conclusion that the Chinese people were drunk with liberty: each military leader and each province was going its own way.

In June and July of 1913 the situation worsened. The southern provinces, where hopes for genuine democracy had been highest, began to declare independence from the government. Yuan, who had been very careful to place his own supporters in key military posts, quickly gained the upper hand in the fighting that ensued. Those of his opponents who survived were forced to flee the country. Sun, who had been elected provisional president less than two years before, also had to abandon his beloved homeland.

Despite the fact that he was now a political exile, Sun still enjoyed immense prestige as the former president of China. He took refuge in Japan, where public opinion was highly sympathetic toward him and where he could still count on the support of some pan-Asianists. As the tattered remnants of the Chinese United League began to coalesce around him, Sun became determined to establish a new, clandestine revolutionary organization under strong centralized leadership — his own. The organization's objective would be to overthrow Yuan and then take charge of China until such time as a democratic constitution had been devised and decreed.

To those among his revolutionary colleagues who objected to Sun's insistence that all who joined the new organization (which was known as the Chinese Revolutionary party) swear allegiance to him personally as well as to the party program, Sun responded forcefully and directly. He expressed his conviction that his autocratic rule of the party would not be incompatible with the party's democratic aims, that "no matter what the party, all must be obedient to the dictates of the party chief. And how much truer this is in the case of a revolutionary party which has to be obedient in carrying out military commands."

The Chinese revolution cannot be said to aim at liberty. The individual should not have too much liberty, but the nation must have complete liberty of action.
—SUN YAT-SEN

During the period between the early debates concerning the broad outlines of the new party's program and the final resolutions on that program (which were made in July 1914), Sun's views on the merits of autocracy as a political tool became increasingly pronounced. He discarded his previous intention to have the party rule China on a transitional basis. Following the seizure of power, he declared, the party would rule indefinitely. As Sun himself defined it, the new order in China would be one of "government by tutelage."

In August 1914, just weeks after the founding of the Chinese Revolutionary party, international attention was diverted from the course of events in China by the outbreak of World War I. Austria-Hungary had declared war on Serbia on July 28, and Serbia's ally, Russia, mobilized its forces along the German and Austrian frontiers on July 29. Germany then declared war on Russia on August 1 and on France, Russia's ally, on August 3. When Germany then announced that it would not respect Belgian neutrality on the march into France, Britain, which was allied with Belgium, declared war on Germany.

The outbreak of hostilities between the major colonial powers of Europe had immediate repercussions in China, whose technical neutrality in the conflict did not protect her from its effects. Japan, which had concluded an alliance with Great Britain before the war began, declared war on Germany on August 23 and immediately captured Germany's holdings in the Shandong Peninsula, occupying almost half the province. The Japanese government then refused to return the captured territories to China, claiming that it was not obliged to do so since it had won them on the battlefield.

The occupation of Shandong was soon revealed to have been but the first action in a wider Japanese effort to compromise Chinese sovereignty. In January 1915 Japanese diplomats visited Yuan Shikai and presented him with a list of demands that reflected their government's determination to make Japan the leading imperialist power in China. In addition to demanding the enhancement and extension of its existing privileges in China, Japan ordered Yuan Shikai to appoint Japanese political, military, and financial advisers to positions in China's central government. The Japanese also requested the creation of a joint Chinese-Japanese police force for the entire country.

When the substance of the Japanese demands was published, China was convulsed by a nationwide upsurge of anti-Japanese agitation. China's diplomats had little difficulty in persuading Japan's allies among the foreign powers to put pressure on the Japanese government, which duly modified its position. Although the agreement reached between the Chinese and Japanese governments on May 9, 1915, allowed Japan some extension of commercial privileges, it would later be revealed to have been immensely damaging to Japan's long-term interests. As Harold Schiffrin writes, "by reviving the old

Having completed the task of bringing about a political revolution, I am now directing my thought and energies to the reconstruction of the country in its social, industrial, and commercial conditions.
—SUN YAT-SEN
after resigning as president of the provisional government

imperialist tactics in the most heavy-handed and brutal manner, Japan touched off a new, volatile and uncompromising phase of Chinese nationalism, with herself as its chief target. Japan would retain this distinction for most of the next thirty years."

In October 1915 Sun, whose hatred of Yuan Shi-kai was so intense that he had been offering the Japanese political, economic, and military tutelage in China in exchange for their support, made a momentous decision with regard to his personal life: he decided to remarry. His bride, Soong Ching-ling, was to become an important political figure in her own right. Her father, Charles Soong, was a powerful, wealthy Chinese businessman who had worked with Sun during the latter's brief incumbency as director of national railroad planning. A graduate of Wesleyan College in Georgia, Ching-ling was an attractive, thoroughly cosmopolitan young woman who spoke perfect English and read French. She was 23 years old when she married Sun, who was 26 years her senior.

Sun (center, behind boy) at a meeting held in Tokyo, April 1916, to denounce Yuan Shi-kai. Despite Yuan's March declaration that he was not going to make himself emperor, opposition to his brutal regime continued.

The army of the new Republic of China on the march in Beijing in 1915. Yuan Shikai shocked the republic when he accepted a list of demands issued by the Japanese, who essentially wanted to place China under Japanese imperial control.

Sun's first wife, Lu Szu, was still alive, however, and living in Macao. For Sun, who was a Christian, to have openly divorced her in order to marry Ching-ling (who was also a Christian) would have raised a tremendous outcry among the foreign and Chinese Christian communities. According to native Chinese tradition, however, it was perfectly permissible for a man to have more than one wife. So Sun simply married Ching-ling without divorcing his first wife. The considerable social significance of this compromise is explained by Chinese writer Tung Chang and British writer Jon Halliday in their book *Mme Sun Yat-sen*: "At the beginning of the century there was no such thing in China as formal divorce in the generally understood present-day sense of the term. Sun [had] had two alternatives. One was to take Ching-ling as a concubine. The other was to dismiss his wife with a reason which would have involved great humiliation for her. Clearly both were impossible. So what happened is that Sun and his wife created a sort of precedent in Chinese marriage practice, by coming to an amicable arrangement for a permanent separation."

In the fall of 1915, while Sun was in Japan, internal opposition to Yuan Shikai, who had handed down his verdict on democracy by abolishing the National Assembly in 1914, became greatly intensified. On January 1, 1916, five years to the day after the founding of the troubled Chinese Republic, Yuan declared a new dynasty and began to make plans for his coronation. It soon became apparent, however, that he had completely misjudged the mood of the Chinese people. His announcement provoked outrage and hostility in many quarters. The more educated sectors of the population were now convinced that Yuan was completely out of touch with reality. Republican ideas had gained a measure of acceptance in mandarin circles, and several provincial administrations withdrew their support from Yuan. Within a matter of months, Yuan's top bureaucrats and military men were deserting him in droves. Defections from his dictatorial regime continued even when he announced — on March 22, 1916 — that he would not make himself emperor.

Yuan Shikai's brutal campaign against his political opponents forced Sun to flee to Japan, where he organized the first Chinese Revolutionary party in July 1914 and was elected general director. Here Sun (front, center) poses for a group photo with other members when the organization was formed.

Yuan's position finally became completely untenable one month later, when (at the urging of the Japanese) the international commission that was responsible for administering China's salt tax announced its intention to withhold the revenues due the Chinese government. Yuan was thus left bankrupt. In June 1916 Yuan Shikai died, worn out by disappointment and frustration.

Yuan's death did little to relieve the condition of near-anarchy into which China was descending. Although there was general agreement that China's problems could never be solved by the reintroduction of the dynastic system, there was no agreement as to what form of government would best aid her recovery. Yuan was replaced by another general, who also proved incapable of uniting the country, and there began a turbulent 10-year period during which cliques of regional military commanders, known as warlords, struggled for power.

With Yuan dead, Sun returned to China and lived in Guangzhou, where he enjoyed the protection of a friendly southern warlord. Sun hoped to make Guangzhou a model city and to establish a true Chinese republic comprising the southern provinces of Guangdong, Guangxi and Yunnan, but his endeavors to this end were not to be rewarded. The southern warlords, jealous of their own powers and privileges, proved incapable of cooperating with each other. In June 1918, following a brief and unsuccessful visit to Japan, Sun retired to the French quarter in Shanghai, where he would live for the next two years, quietly analyzing his past failures and reshaping and refining his program for China's recovery.

Zhang Zuolin, a chieftain of the northern warlords. After Yuan Shikai's death in June 1916, control of the government passed into the hands of northern warlords, many of whom had been Yuan Shikai's generals.

Early in 1919 China witnessed the greatest explosion of nationalist protest in its history. World War I had ended with Germany's defeat in November 1918, and representatives of the victorious Allied powers (France, Great Britain, the United States, and Italy) gathered in Paris in January 1919 for a conference that was intended to negotiate a final settlement between all the nations that had participated in the conflict or been affected by it. China, which had entered the war on the Allied side in 1917, had great hopes that the conference would negotiate a just peace, one in keeping with U.S. President Woodrow Wilson's contention that the war had been fought to put an end to power politics.

In April 1919 the Allied powers formally endorsed Japan's occupation of the Shandong Peninsula. The Chinese people were horrified at this betrayal of their hopes by the very nations for whom thousands of Chinese coolies had labored in Europe during the war. Their consternation became even more pro-

Members of an army unit loyal to the government in Guangzhou led by Sun. In June 1922 Sun was driven out of Guangzhou by the warlord Chen Jiongming.

found when it was revealed that the government in Beijing had secretly assured Japan in September 1918 that it would recognize Japan's claim to the peninsula.

On May 4, 1919, more than 3,000 angry students marched in Beijing to protest the Allied decision and their own government's complicity in that decision. In the wake of the Beijing demonstration, anti-Japanese boycotts and demonstrations were staged throughout China. The government in Beijing capitulated a month later, announcing that the Chinese delegation to the peace conference would not accept the Allied decision and would refuse to sign the final peace treaty. Further evidence of the extent to which the government had been shaken by the popular response to its secret dealings with Japan came when the government dismissed several pro-Japanese officials and freed the more than 1,000 students it had imprisoned.

In November 1920 Guangzhou was captured by a friendly warlord named Chen Jiongming, and Sun was invited to return. Although many of the southern warlords considered Sun a valuable ally in terms of his high reputation, none of them were prepared to share power with him or to institute reforms that reflected his political beliefs. Sun was able, however, to begin to reestablish a power base of his own.

Sun's primary ambition at this point in his career was to mount a military expedition from Guangzhou and then to march north to capture Beijing, thus unifying the country. He persuaded the ambitious Chen Jiongming to assist him, and in 1921 the "Northern Expedition" got under way. Early in 1922, however, Chen and Sun had a major disagreement concerning policy priorities. Sun managed to oust Chen, but in June 1922 Chen counterattacked and drove Sun out of Guangzhou. The confusion of warlord politics in southern China was repeated throughout the country. Governments rose and fell so rapidly that it was difficult to keep track of them.

Another momentous consequence of World War I was the Russian Revolution, which particularly interested those Chinese who were groping for some solution to their own country's terrible problems. Before the revolution Russia had been a backward, agrarian nation ruled by an autocratic emperor. After the revolution Russia was reconstituted by its new communist rulers as a workers' state — the Soviet Union — and seemed to make rapid progress toward modernization and increased social justice. The Chinese thought that if Russia could reform, then China might, too. As they studied the revolution, many Chinese, particularly radical students, became convinced that the ideas of Marx and Lenin might also be the key to the creation of a new social and political order in China. Chinese radicals increasingly came to feel that Western liberal ideas were irrelevant, promising at best only a gradual change, and not the rapid transformation that would end the suffering of the Chinese people. In July 1921 the Chinese Communist party (CCP) was founded by a group of the most radical leftists in the country.

While many Chinese found developments in the Soviet Union a hopeful sign, most Western governments were violently opposed to the new state, whose communist leaders advocated world revolution. Shortly after the revolution, over 50,000 Allied troops — British, American, Italian, Serbian, Czech, Polish, French, and Japanese — invaded Soviet territory and conducted operations in support of Russian counterrevolutionary groups. The Soviet leaders in turn saw in the European-dominated areas of Asia a possibility of seriously damaging the economic interests of the unfriendly European powers at little cost or risk. Thus, the Soviet Union selectively undertook to sponsor national revolutions in Asia, particularly in China.

During the difficult years from 1913 to 1922, Sun had hoped for much more from the Western powers than had actually been forthcoming. His requests for their assistance in building a truly democratic and republican China had always been rebuffed. He was regarded as either an impractical dreamer or a dangerous radical whose ideas might end foreign influence in China. Thus it came about that Sun finally turned to the Soviet Union for assistance.

EASTFOTO

Sun attending a memorial service for Russian revolutionary leader Vladimir Lenin, whom he had held in high esteem. In an obituary message Sun called Lenin "a superb politician and a leader of ingenuity."

7

Threshold of Victory

The Soviets were glad to supply both aid and advice to Sun, even though Sun made it clear that while he wanted Soviet assistance, he considered communism unsuitable for China. Sun felt that Marx's bleak predictions of the inevitability of class war and revolution in modern industrial societies were not relevant to China, which was at a preindustrial stage of development, and that China's situation called for a more humane, less doctrinaire form of socialism than that espoused by the Soviet leadership.

The chief Soviet adviser to Sun, a veteran revolutionary named Mikhail Borodin, arrived in China in October 1923. Borodin, who had briefly taught school in Chicago while living in the United States, immediately set to work to assist Sun in creating a modern, sophisticated, and powerful political and military organization — a new incarnation of the Guomindang.

The overwhelming problem facing Sun and the Guomindang was the continuing military supremacy of the warlords. Sun had never commanded a reliable military force, having had to make do throughout his career to date with mercenaries like the Roving Braves or self-seeking southern warlords

In a nutshell, it is my idea to make capitalism create socialism in China, so that these two economic forces of human evolution will work side by side in future civilization.
—SUN YAT-SEN

Portrait of Sun Yat-sen. After Yuan Shikai's death, Sun settled in Guangzhou under the protection of a southern warlord, but by 1923, convinced China needed a final break with the military order, he turned to the Soviet Union for help.

like Chen Jiongming, all of whom had failed him. In 1924, with Soviet assistance and advice, the Guomindang established its own military academy, at Huangpu Island, near Guangzhou. The academy was intended to produce young professional military officers, motivated by nationalism and educated in radical political thought.

Following the pattern first established by the Soviet army, the leadership of Huangpu was split between two men. A CCP member named Zhou Enlai assumed responsibility for political indoctrination, while military training was supervised by a professional soldier named Chiang Kai-shek, who had studied military science in Japan and in the Soviet Union. It was while studying in the Soviet Union that Chiang came to acquire his immense dislike of communism and his distrust of Soviet methods and intentions in China. (Chiang would later marry Soong Mei-ling, the youngest of Charles Soong's three daughters. Mei-ling, like Sun's wife, Ching-ling, was American-educated.)

Mikhail Borodin in Hankow, China, addressing a crowd with his student interpreter in 1927. The Soviet Union happily complied with Sun's request for aid and advice; Borodin arrived in China in 1923 to consult with Sun on the problems facing China.

Borodin, who was advising the CCP as well as Sun's Guomindang, wanted to see the two groups cooperate in the interests of Chinese nationalism. Both the CCP and the Guomindang agreed on the need for a strong, centralized Chinese government capable of neutralizing the warlords and reducing foreign influence. But the two organizations' views on the kind of social and economic order that was to be established in China once national unity had been achieved were completely incompatible. Sun nevertheless decided to permit CCP members to enter the Guomindang.

With the help of the Communist party of China, Sun founded the Huangpu Military Academy to train the revolutionary armed forces. This photo shows Sun, general director of the academy, and Madame Soong Chingling at the inaugural ceremony of the academy on June 16, 1924.

99

Zhou Enlai played a major role in training professional revolutionaries for the Chinese Communist party (CCP). Like Sun, Zhou also traveled to Japan and studied political theory there.

The Soviet impact on Sun's thought was minimal because of his commitment to both Chinese traditional humanism and Western liberalism. But the Soviet influence on Sun's organizational methods is quite clear. The organizational principles adopted by the newly restructured Guomindang in 1923 were Soviet in origin. The manifesto of the party, enacted in January 1924, called for a party structure modeled directly upon that of the Soviet Communist party. In Sun's plans, China would be dominated by one party led by a highly centralized group.

Sun felt the need for centralized leadership because he believed that China's basic problems were externally induced. He believed that only a strong China could deal with the menace of the foreign powers. Moreover, Sun still doubted the ability of most common Chinese people to govern themselves and remained convinced that an indefinite period of one party would be essential. When we look at the confusion and turmoil that characterized China during Sun's lifetime, his autocratic prescriptions for the alleviation of his country's suffering become more understandable.

The site of the Hubei military government, which was set up after rebels captured the Wuhan cities in 1911. In the foreground is a bronze statue of Sun Yat-sen.

The children of Sun Yat-sen
(pictured from left to right)—
Sun On, Sun Yuen, and Sun
Fo with his wife.

With Soviet advice and assistance, Sun at last began to make great progress. He had a strong political party, an army, and a powerful foreign ally. This was the situation toward which he had worked for almost thirty years. But Sun was now 58 years old, and he had lived a life of constant movement and anxiety. His health, particularly his digestion, had not been good for a long time.

In December 1924 Sun fell ill in Tianjin, where he was conferring with his colleagues. In late January of 1925, exploratory surgery revealed that Sun had cancer of the liver. The disease was so advanced that Sun's condition was declared inoperable. On March 12, 1925, Sun Yat-sen died.

Although Sun was struck down just as it seemed that he would finally realize his dreams, he had built a political and military machine that could continue without him. Sun's heirs, both Communists and Nationalists, carried his work forward.

I was born with the poor and am still poor.
—SUN YAT-SEN
at the end of his life

8

Sun Yat-sen's Legacy

Though Sun was dead, his dream of a unified China lived on. The Guomindang was governed by Sun's comrades and allies. His brother-in-law, Chiang Kai-shek, emerged as its military leader. The Huangpu cadets whom Chiang had trained became the core of the new Nationalist army. Chiang followed Sun's precepts of centralized control and personal ties between the followers and their leader, creating a group of very loyal officers.

The immediate problem facing the Guomindang was that which had for so long faced Sun: the disunity engendered by warlord rule. The Guomindang's projected solution to the problem had also been Sun's: to mount an expedition to the north and unify the country by force. The Guomindang saw the problem as primarily a military one, but the Communists, following Marxist political philosophy, looked first to economic problems, and sought ways of winning over disaffected social groups. At first, the two parties made an effective combination. The Communists provided propagandists and political agitators who worked carefully with such groups as peasants, workers, and women to prepare the way for the Guomindang army.

In July 1926 the Northern Expedition set out from Guangzhou. There was much hard fighting, particularly at the beginning of the campaign. As the com-

Peace, struggle, save China.
—reportedly Sun Yat-sen's last words

The Great Wall of China was built by the first emperor of imperial China, Chin Shih Huang-ti, in the 3rd century B.C. to protect China from invading northern nomads. A Chinese proverb says: "Chin Shih Huang-ti is dead, but the wall still stands."

Thousands of Chinese turned out to greet Nationalist troops when they entered Shanghai in April 1927 after their success against the northern warlords' military forces.

bined Guomindang and Communist forces moved north, however, many warlords saw the wisdom of joining them. By the time the Northern Expedition reached the Changjiang River in the spring of 1927, 34 warlord armies had been absorbed.

Once the south and center of China was firmly under Guomindang control, victory was not far off. Now that the end of the revolution was in sight, the question of the future suddenly became important. Who was to rule? Was there to be only political revolution to unite China, as the Guomindang intended? Or would there also be a social revolution to raise up the peasants and workers as the Communists wanted?

Either side would eventually have turned upon the other, but the Guomindang struck first. While the Communists were being ordered by the Soviet leader, Joseph Stalin, to cooperate with Chiang, Chiang attacked them. The fighting began in Shanghai in April 1927. Chiang's forces slaughtered tens of thousands of Communists and their sympathizers. A long civil war had begun.

When they were driven into the rural areas, the Communist leaders found themselves forced to listen to the ideas of a young peasant organizer, Mao Zedong. Mao had long been saying that a communist revolution in China had to be based in the countryside, upon the power of the peasants, and not among the industrial working class, as orthodox Soviet Marxist-Leninist principles suggested. Thus, while Chiang Kai-shek formed a Nationalist government, Mao and the Communists began years of work among the peasantry, often fleeing their rural bases just ahead of the Guomindang armies.

Chiang Kai-shek's Nationalist party was never to be able to unite China, though it declared itself the legitimate government of the country and attracted international acceptance. Chiang's organization remained largely military and never became a mass-based party. It was also strongly authoritarian. It faced great poverty, backwardness, and underdevelopment in rural China, but proposed no remedies. The Communists, addressing the need for sweeping social and economic change, won the allegiance of the peasant masses.

Chiang and the Guomindang also faced external threats. Japan captured additional areas of China, taking economically rich Manchuria in 1931. Chiang was slow to fight Japan, seeing the Communists as the greater danger. This permitted the Communists, who called for immediate resistance, to seize the banner of Chinese nationalism.

Finally, the Sino-Japanese conflict widened and became part of World War II in 1941. For a brief period, the Communists, now led by Mao Zedong, and the Nationalists of Chiang Kai-shek cooperated once again. But even the defeat of Japan in 1945 scarcely interrupted the struggle between the two great Chinese political parties.

AP/WIDE WORLD PHOTOS

After Sun Yat-sen's death in March 1925, it was General Chiang Kai-shek who led the Nationalist army to victory over the warlords who had divided up China. Chiang Kai-shek formally unified China by 1928; however, he ruled it under a military dictatorship.

Mrs. H. H. Kung, Mrs. Sun Yat-sen, and Mrs. Chiang Kai-shek (left to right). The three sisters of the Soong family are shown inspecting the ruins of homes that were destroyed in the Japanese air raids as the Sino-Japanese War widened in 1940.

UPI/BETTMANN NEWSPHOTOS

Communist soldiers standing guard in Shanghai in 1949 while civilians view part of the large quantity of war supplies left behind by Chiang and the Nationalists who, at the close of the second civil war, fled to Taiwan.

If when I die I am still a dictator I will certainly go down into the oblivion of all dictators. If on the other hand I succeed in establishing a truly stable foundation for a democratic government, I will live forever in every home in China.

— CHIANG KAI-SHEK
Chinese Nationalist leader

After the Japanese defeat in 1945, and despite the fact that it received enormous amounts of American aid and advice, the Guomindang was unable to overcome its own internal corruption and the terrible economic problems facing China. The inability of the Guomindang to put an end to the vicious economic decline made the Chinese currency totally worthless. This angered even China's middle classes and increased support for the Communists. Open civil war began once more in 1947. Popular support and organizational ability gave the Communists victory over the militarily superior, but demoralized, Nationalists.

Riding the twin programs of social revolution and opposition to Japan, Mao had achieved success and popularity where Chiang found failure. Chiang and the battered remnants of the Nationalist army fled to Taiwan in May 1949. On October 1, 1949, Mao Zedong and the Chinese Communist party proclaimed the establishment of the People's Republic of China. To the Communists, this was the successful completion of the Chinese revolutionary process that had begun with the revolution of 1911.

Today, the Communists rule the mainland from Beijing, and the Nationalists rule Taiwan from Taipei. Almost all the nations of the world, including the United States, now recognize the government in Beijing as the sole, legitimate government of all of China. But Taiwan is very strong economically and very modern compared to the mainland, which remains poor and backward.

The two Chinese governments and their followers disagree on many things, including the nature of Chinese history. But they are in rare agreement on the importance and character of Dr. Sun Yat-sen. Both agree that Sun was the preeminent figure of the early stages of the Chinese revolution. The historical contribution of Mao Zedong is currently being debated in China because, late in life, he instigated a period of political upheaval that may have set back China's economic and political development for decades. The government of Taiwan remains fiercely anticommunist and has enshrined Sun as the founder of modern China. Therefore, Sun Yat-sen stands out as the most important Chinese political leader of the 20th century.

The Chinese have a saying, "Heroes are Heaven-born," which suggests that great leaders are not made of the same clay as the rest of us, that they are supernatural in some respects. But we know that all great leaders, when their history is closely examined, are revealed as all too human. Sun Yat-sen was a very capable man, always learning from his experience and his wide reading. Above all, he was a determined man, never flagging in his efforts to see his country free and safe from internal discord and foreign threats.

During Sun's lifetime China was at a turning point in her history. The Chinese tradition had out-lived its usefulness, and the Chinese people wanted an infusion of outside ideas and institutions. This process was bound to be painful and confusing. Sun was rarely able to follow a fixed course in his political principles or his program. He had to get his allies where he could, be it in expansionist Japan, colonialist France, or the revolutionary Soviet Union.

Sun learned from both the Chinese tradition and the modern world. He was very much a product of his era, a man uneasily balanced between the old and the new, between East and West, just as was China itself. Today his contribution is recognized by Chinese the world over, who refer to him as "Guo-fu"—the Father of the Country.

XINHUA NEWS AGENCY

Chairman Mao Zedong in 1949. Mao led the Communist army that defeated Chiang Kai-shek's Nationalist forces. On October 1, 1949, the Communists proclaimed the establishment of the People's Republic of China.

Further Reading

Barlow, Jeffrey G. *Sun Yat-sen and the French, 1900–1908.* Berkeley: University of California Institute of East Asian Studies, 1979.

Clubb, O. Edmund. *20th Century China.* New York: Columbia University Press, 1978.

Jansen, Marius B. *The Japanese and Sun Yat-sen.* Stanford: Stanford University Press, 1954.

Seagrave, Sterling. *The Soong Dynasty.* New York: Harper & Row Publishers, 1985.

Schiffrin, Harold Z. *Sun Yat-sen and the Origins of the Chinese Revolution.* Berkeley: University of California Press, 1968.

———. *Sun Yat-sen: Reluctant Revolutionary.* Boston: Little, Brown and Company, 1980.

Spence, Jonathan D. *The Gate of Heavenly Peace.* New York: The Viking Press, 1981.

Wilbur, C. Martin. *Sun Yat-sen: Frustrated Patriot.* New York: Columbia University Press, 1976.

Chronology

Nov. 12, 1866	Sun Yat-sen born in Guangdong province
1879–83	Studies in Hawaii
1887–92	Attends the Hong Kong Medical College
1894	Sun founds the Revive China Society in Hawaii
1895	China loses Sino-Japanese War
	Sun plans uprising in Guangzhou; flees to Japan when uprising is uncovered
1896	Goes to London to study; is kidnapped and briefly held in the Chinese Embassy
1898	Founds the revolutionary publication *China Mail* in Japan
1899	Anti-imperialist Boxer Rebellion breaks out
1900	Sun directs Huizhou antigovernment rebellion in October
1904	Tours United States working with Chinese-American anti-monarchical "secret societies"
1905	Founds the Chinese United League and the *People's Journal* in Tokyo
1907	Directs four uprisings in southern China from the League's headquarters in French Indochina
1911	Successful uprising in Wuhan
Jan. 1, 1912	Sun Yat-sen inaugurated provisional president of the Republic of China
February 1912	Resigns presidency in favor of the warlord Yuan Shikai
August 1912	The Chinese United League becomes the Guomindang, or Nationalist party
1913	Sun participates in unsuccessful revolt of five southern provinces against Yuan; flees to Japan
June 1916	Yuan Shikai dies
1921	Sun attempts unsuccessful "Northern Expedition" to unify China
	Chinese Communist party founded
1923	Sun accepts Soviet assistance for the Guomindang
March 12, 1925	Sun Yat-sen dies of cancer in Beijing
1949	Chinese Communists proclaim the founding of the People's Republic of China

Index

Jeffrey G. Barlow holds a Ph.D. in history from the
University of California, Berkeley. He is currently
Chairman and Associate Professor in the Department
of History at Lewis & Clark College, in Portland, Ore-
gon. He is the author of *Sun Yat-sen and the French,
1900–1908*, and co-author (with his wife, Christine
Richardson) of *China Doctor of John Day*. He lived in
south China and Taiwan for a number of years.

Arthur M. Schlesinger, jr., taught history at Harvard
for many years and is currently Albert Schweitzer Professor of the Humanities at City University of New
York. He is the author of numerous highly praised
works in American history and has twice been
awarded the Pulitzer Prize. He served in the White
House as special assistant to Presidents Kennedy and
Johnson.